W9-BGO-422

Programmer's Guide to Drupal

Jennifer Hodgdon

O'REILLY®

Beijing · Cambridge · Farnham · Köln · Sebastopol · Tokyo

Programmer's Guide to Drupal

by Jennifer Hodgdon

Published by O'Reilly Media, Inc., 1005 Gravenstein Highway North, Sebastopol, CA 95472.

O'Reilly books may be purchased for educational, business, or sales promotional use. Online editions are also available for most titles (*http://my.safaribooksonline.com*). For more information, contact our corporate/institutional sales department: 800-998-9938 or *corporate@oreilly.com*.

Editor: Meghan Blanchette	**Proofreader:** Mary Ellen Smith
Production Editor: Melanie Yarbrough	**Cover Designer:** Karen Montgomery
	Interior Designer: David Futato
	Illustrator: Rebecca Demarest

December 2012:   First Edition

Revision History for the First Edition:

2012-12-06   First release

See *http://oreilly.com/catalog/errata.csp?isbn=9781449343316* for release details.

ISBN: 978-1-449-34331-6

[LSI]

Table of Contents

Preface

Welcome! This book is meant to launch you into the world of programming with the open-source web content management system known as *Drupal*. Hopefully, with the aid of this book, you will pass smoothly through the stage of being a novice Drupal programmer, while avoiding making the mistakes that many expert Drupal programmers made in their first Drupal programming endeavors. If you make an effort to learn the "Drupal Way" of programming and follow the guidelines in this book, you can look forward to many enjoyable and fruitful years of programming with Drupal.

Intended Audience

This book was written primarily for people with a background in programming who are new to using and programming with Drupal. If you fit this profile, the main reason to read this book is that whatever your programming background, your experiences have taught you certain lessons—and only some of them apply well to Drupal. This book aims to make you aware of which lessons are which, and help you make a successful transition to being an expert Drupal programmer: someone who knows just how and where to apply your programming skills to have the greatest effect.

This book should also be useful for the following audiences:

- Anyone working with Drupal who wants to understand how it works "under the hood."
- Drupal site builders and themers who have realized they need to do some programming for customization, and want to do it "the Drupal way."
- Drupal users who want to contribute to the Drupal open-source project by programming.

The backend of Drupal and most of its code is written in PHP, utilizing some variety of SQL for database queries. Accordingly, this book concentrates on PHP and database programming for Drupal, although there are definitely opportunities to program in Flash, JavaScript, and other frontend languages with Drupal.

Because this book was written for a programming audience, it assumes knowledge of the following:

- The basics of the Web and HTTP requests.
- The basics of PHP programming and programming in general (standard programming terminology is not explained).

See "Where to Find More Information" (page vii) to find resources about these topics, if you need additional background.

How to Use This Book

In order to get the most out of this book, I would suggest that you start by reading Chapter 1 and making sure you are familiar with all the material in it. If you have never installed Drupal at all or tried to use it, you should definitely also do that now (there are installation instructions in the *INSTALL.txt* file that comes with Drupal, or at *http://drupal.org/documentation/install*).

After that, you should be ready to start looking at some Drupal programming examples, so I would suggest that you download the *Examples for Developers* project from *http://drupal.org/project/examples*, which is a comprehensive set of programming examples covering *Drupal core* (the base Drupal system, not including add-on modules). The Examples project is maintained by many contributors within the Drupal community, and it is an excellent resource; its existence has allowed this book to concentrate on the background information you will need to become a Drupal programming expert and on giving examples that are beyond the scope of the Examples project.

The next step I'd suggest would be to install one or two of the example modules from the Examples project, try them out, and then look through their code (check the *README.txt* file for installation instructions). If there's a programming topic that you're particularly interested in, you could choose an example module on that basis; I would particularly recommend the Block and Page example modules as good general starting points. Keep in mind when you are reviewing the code that the official Drupal API reference site, *http://api.drupal.org*, is the best place to go to find documentation on particular Drupal API functions.

That should give you a little bit of experience looking at Drupal code, at which point I would suggest returning to this book and reading Chapter 2 and Chapter 3 carefully, to learn about the dos and don'ts of Drupal programming. At that point, you should have the necessary background for the special topics and examples of Chapter 4, and to return to the Examples for Developers project and look at examples there of interest; skim them so you know what's there, and then come back to individual topics and examples when you need them.

Finally, Chapter 5 offers a few closing tips and suggestions, and many sections of this book have suggestions for further reading.

Drupal Versions

Every few years, the Drupal project releases a new *major version* of Drupal (Drupal 6, Drupal 7, and so on). Each major version of Drupal brings large, incompatible changes to the architecture and API, and generally, programming that you do for one major version cannot be used without modification in other major versions. *Contributed modules* (additional modules downloaded from drupal.org) also make large, incompatible architectural and API changes with their releases (Views 6.x-2.x versus 6.x-3.x, for instance).

The code samples in this book are compatible with Drupal 7, and with particular Drupal 7 versions of contributed modules as noted in their sections. The descriptive sections of this book are also written primarily with Drupal 7 in mind, with notes about changes expected in Drupal 8 (which was still in development as of this writing).

Where to Find More Information

Drupal Site Building and General Drupal Information

When I started using and programming with Drupal, there weren't really any books available on using Drupal to build websites, so I don't have any specific general Drupal book recommendations; the Drupal project maintains a list of current books about Drupal at *http://drupal.org/books*.

Here is a list of online resources on site building and the Drupal project in general:

http://drupal.org/documentation
> The Drupal Community Documentation, a wiki-like compendium of pages about nearly everything in Drupal (installation, site building, programming, etc.). It has a lot of coverage, but since it is open to editing by all members of the Drupal community, it is of varying quality and only somewhat organized. Within this documentation, the "Developing for Drupal" section and the "Theming" section are of most use to programmers; other sections are aimed at setting up sites with Drupal, configuring modules, and the like.

http://drupal.org/planet
> Drupal Planet, which is an aggregated feed composed of many Drupal-related blogs. Subscribe to keep up-to-date on new developments in Drupal and to read blog posts on programming topics.

http://groups.drupal.org
> Central place to find topical and geographical Drupal groups, each of which has a forum. Many of them also have meetings and events (online or in-person) that you can attend.

http://drupal.org/irc
> The Drupal community uses IRC for online chatting, and this section of the Drupal website contains a channel list and background information.

http://association.drupal.org
> Website of the Drupal Association, the nonprofit organization behind the Drupal project.

http://drupal.org/project/modules and http://drupal.org/project/themes
> Search for downloads of contributed Drupal modules and themes here.

Drupal Programming Reference and Background

The Drupal API changes often enough that if someone tried to write an API reference book, it would probably be outdated before it was published. So, the following online resources are recommended (in addition, some of the general Drupal resources of the previous section have programming information):

http://api.drupal.org
> The API reference site for Drupal. As of this writing, this site only includes Drupal core and a few contributed modules; *http://drupalcontrib.org* is a similar reference site that includes all of the Drupal contributed modules. Use one of these sites to find documentation about a specific Drupal function, class, or constant whose name you know. See "Using api.drupal.org" (page 97) for more information.

http://drupal.org/developing/api
> Tutorials and conceptual explanations for the various Drupal APIs. Use this reference if you do not know what function you need to use, or if you need more background information.

http://drupal.org/project/examples
> The Examples for Developers project, which is a set of well-documented example modules that aim to illustrate all of the core Drupal APIs. There has been some discussion about distributing these examples as part of the Drupal core download, but as of this writing, they are still a separate project.

http://drupal.org/writing-secure-code
> Documentation about writing secure code in Drupal. Also, Greg James Knaddison, one of the prominent members of the Drupal Security Team, has written *Cracking Drupal: A Drop in the Bucket* (John Wiley and Sons), which is widely considered to be the definitive reference for Drupal security.

http://drupal.org/coding-standards
> The coding standards for the Drupal project.

http://drupal.org/new-contributors
> A list of tasks for people with a variety of skill sets, with step-by-step instructions, suitable for people who are new to contributing to the Drupal project.

http://drupal.org/novice
> Detailed instructions on how to contribute *patches* (code fixes) to Drupal.

PHP Resources

There are hundreds of books about PHP, and everyone should be able to find one that suits their needs, background, and style preferences. For an experienced programmer who is new to PHP, I recommend:

- *PHP in a Nutshell* (*http://oreil.ly/PHP_nutshell*) by Paul Hudson (O'Reilly) to learn the PHP language.

- *Web Database Applications with PHP and MySQL* (*http://oreil.ly/web_db_apps_PHP_MySQL*) by Hugh E. Williams and David Lane (O'Reilly) to learn the basics of web applications with PHP, including security concerns and how all the pieces fit together.

- For reference information about specific PHP functions, *http://php.net* (that is always the most up-to-date reference; you can also download the entire reference for local or offline access).

Database Resources

Drupal can run on a variety of databases; most commonly, people use either MySQL, a MySQL clone such as MariaDB, or PostgreSQL. If you program with Drupal, you will need to use the Drupal Database API for maximum portability rather than writing MySQL or other database queries directly. Because of this, websites and references aimed at specific databases are of limited use to Drupal programmers. Instead, I recommend:

- *Web Database Applications with PHP and MySQL* (previously mentioned) as a good starting point for learning the basics of queries useful for web programming.

- *SQL Pocket Guide* (*http://oreil.ly/SQL_Pocket_Guide*) by Jonathan Gennick (O'Reilly), which highlights the similarities and differences between the various databases' query syntax and capabilities.

Other Web Technology Resources

Again, *Web Database Applications with PHP and MySQL* is a good starting point for learning about how the web server, PHP scripting language, database, and browser interact in web applications in general. For reference on HTML, CSS, and JavaScript, I recommend:

- *http://www.w3schools.com* has a great online reference for HTML and CSS.
- If you prefer a book format, the O'Reilly pocket references are handy: *CSS Pocket Reference* (*http://oreil.ly/CSS_Pocket_Ref_4*) by Eric A. Meyer and *HTML & XHTML Pocket Reference* (*http://oreil.ly/HTML_XHTML_Pocket_Ref_4*) by Jennifer Niederst Robbins.
- For JavaScript, I am continually pulling out my well-worn copy of *JavaScript: The Definitive Guide* (*http://oreil.ly/JS_Definitive*) (O'Reilly), which contains both the basics of JavaScript programming and an API reference.
- Drupal makes extensive use of the jQuery JavaScript library, which has a comprehensive online API reference at *http://docs.jquery.com*.

Conventions Used in This Book

The following terminology conventions are used in this book:

- While on some operating systems directories are called "folders," this book always refers to them as "directories."
- Sample site URLs use "example.com" as the base site URL.
- Sample modules have machine name `'mymodule'`, and sample themes have machine name `'mytheme'`.

The following typographical conventions are used in this book:

Italic
: Indicates new terms, URLs, email addresses, filenames, and file extensions.

`Constant width`
: Used for program listings, as well as within paragraphs to refer to program elements such as variable or function names, databases, data types, environment variables, statements, and keywords.

Constant width bold

Shows commands or other text that should be typed literally by the user.

Constant width italic

Shows text that should be replaced with user-supplied values or by values determined by context.

 This icon signifies a tip, suggestion, or general note.

 This icon indicates a warning or caution.

Using Code Examples

This book is here to help you get your job done. In general, if this book includes code examples, you may use the code in this book in your programs and documentation. You do not need to contact us for permission unless you're reproducing a significant portion of the code. For example, writing a program that uses several chunks of code from this book does not require permission. Selling or distributing a CD-ROM of examples from O'Reilly books does require permission. Answering a question by citing this book and quoting example code does not require permission. Incorporating a significant amount of example code from this book into your product's documentation does require permission.

We appreciate, but do not require, attribution. An attribution usually includes the title, author, publisher, and ISBN. For example: "*Programmer's Guide to Drupal* by Jennifer Hodgdon (O'Reilly). Copyright 2013 Poplar Productivityware, LLC., 978-1-449-34331-6."

If you feel your use of code examples falls outside fair use or the permission given above, feel free to contact us at *permissions@oreilly.com*.

Safari® Books Online

 *Safari Books Online* is an on-demand digital library that delivers expert content in both book and video form from the world's leading authors in technology and business.

Technology professionals, software developers, web designers, and business and creative professionals use Safari Books Online as their primary resource for research, problem solving, learning, and certification training.

Safari Books Online offers a range of product mixes and pricing programs for organizations, government agencies, and individuals. Subscribers have access to thousands of books, training videos, and prepublication manuscripts in one fully searchable database from publishers like O'Reilly Media, Prentice Hall Professional, Addison-Wesley Professional, Microsoft Press, Sams, Que, Peachpit Press, Focal Press, Cisco Press, John Wiley & Sons, Syngress, Morgan Kaufmann, IBM Redbooks, Packt, Adobe Press, FT Press, Apress, Manning, New Riders, McGraw-Hill, Jones & Bartlett, Course Technology, and dozens more. For more information about Safari Books Online, please visit us online.

How to Contact Us

Please address comments and questions concerning this book to the publisher:

O'Reilly Media, Inc.
1005 Gravenstein Highway North
Sebastopol, CA 95472
800-998-9938 (in the United States or Canada)
707-829-0515 (international or local)
707-829-0104 (fax)

We have a web page for this book, where we list errata, examples, and any additional information. You can access this page at *http://oreil.ly/Prog_Guide_Drupal*.

To comment or ask technical questions about this book, send email to *bookques tions@oreilly.com*.

For more information about our books, courses, conferences, and news, see our website at *http://www.oreilly.com*.

Find us on Facebook: *http://facebook.com/oreilly*

Follow us on Twitter: *http://twitter.com/oreillymedia*

Watch us on YouTube: *http://www.youtube.com/oreillymedia*

Acknowledgments

Writing this book would not have been possible without the world-wide Drupal open-source project community, and I would especially like to acknowledge the support of the women of Drupal and the members of the Seattle and Spokane Drupal Groups. Without their help and encouragement, I would never have even gotten in touch with

O'Reilly (thanks Angie!), much less decided to write this book. The daily cheerleading of my partner, Zach Carter, was also a great help in completing it. And all of the contributors to the Examples for Developers project made it possible for this book to concentrate on principles and pitfalls, without the need for it to include as many examples in its pages.

I would also like to thank Will Hartmann (PapaGrande), Michelle Williamson (micnap), Melissa Anderson (eliza411), Katherine Senzee (ksenzee), and Michael J. Ross (mjross) for providing technical reviews of this book.

And finally, I would like to thank my editor at O'Reilly, Meghan Blanchette, for many valuable suggestions, and for patiently guiding me through the publishing process.

CHAPTER 1

Overview of Drupal

What Is Drupal?

Depending on who you talk to, you'll hear Drupal called a *Content Management System* (CMS) or a *Content Management Framework* (CMF, a platform that you can use to build a custom CMS)--and both are accurate. It can be called a basic CMS because after installing only the base Drupal software, you can create a website with forums, static pages, and/or a blog, and manage the content online. On the other hand, it can be called a flexible CMF because most people choose to add additional modules to Drupal in order to build more complicated websites with more features, and Drupal also allows you to create fully custom modules.

Drupal is *free and open-source software* (FOSS), governed by the *GNU General Public License* (GPL) version 2 (or, at your option, any later version). If you have never read the GPL and plan to use Drupal, you would be well advised to do so (even more so if you plan to do any Drupal programming, for yourself or others). The GPL governs not only what you can do with Drupal software itself, but also what you can do with any add-ons you download from drupal.org, code you find on drupal.org documentation pages, and any *derivative work* (work that contains GPL-licensed work, verbatim or with modifications) that you or others create. It's also written in plain English and is quite a good read (for programmer-types anyway); you can find it in the *LICENSE.txt* file distributed with Drupal core, or at *http://gnu.org*.

And finally, Drupal is also a project and a community. Unlike some FOSS software that is developed primarily by one company that later releases the source code to the public, Drupal is continually evolving due to the efforts of a world wide community of individuals and companies who donate their time and money to create and test Drupal software, write the documentation, translate it into other languages, answer support questions, keep the drupal.org web servers running, and organize get-togethers on a local and world wide scale.

Drupal Core

Drupal core is what you get when you download Drupal from *http://drupal.org/project/drupal*, consisting of a set of PHP scripts (some with embedded HTML mark-up), JavaScript, CSS, and other files. This software interacts with a web server (typically, Apache), a database (MySQL, PostgreSQL, and SQLite are supported by Drupal core version 7, and others are supported by add-on modules), and a web browser to provide the basics of a CMS:

- A URL request dispatch system
- A user account management system with flexible permissions and roles
- Online content editing
- A *theme* (template) system, which lets you override how everything from a button to an entire page is displayed
- A *block* system that allows you to place chunks of content in various regions of a site's pages (this system will be quite different in Drupal 8, and more flexible).
- A navigation *menu* builder
- A flexible *taxonomy* system that supports categories, tags, and user-defined taxonomy vocabularies
- Optional modules supporting commenting, content fields, RSS aggregation, search, and site features such as forums and polls (depending on the Drupal version, some of these may require downloading add-on modules instead of being part of Drupal core)
- The ability to set up a site in different languages and translate content (depending on the Drupal version, some add-on modules may be required to make a multilingual or non-English site)
- Logging of system events and errors
- An API for Drupal programmers

Drupal Add-Ons: Modules, Themes, Distributions, and Translations

Drupal is modular software, meaning that you can turn site features and functionality on and off by enabling and disabling *modules*. Drupal core comes with a few required modules and several optional modules; you can download thousands of additional *contributed modules* from *http://drupal.org/project/modules*. Most modules have configuration options that you can modify from the Drupal administration interface, by logging in to the Drupal-based site using an account that has been given appropriate permissions. The permission system is flexible: you can define named *roles*, which are granted specific *permissions* (the permissions are defined by modules), and you can assign one or more roles to each user account.

Drupal uses a *theme* system to separate the content from the specific HTML markup and styling. This means that if you want to redesign the site's layout or styling, you can do so by downloading a new theme from *http://drupal.org/project/themes*, purchasing a commercially available theme, or creating one yourself—once installed and enabled, it takes effect immediately to change the look of your site without the necessity of editing your content pages. The theme system allows you to use the default display for whatever you are happy with and override the parts you want to change; the overrides can be at anything from the lowest level (for example, the presentation of buttons) to the full page.

You can also download Drupal in a *distribution*, which consists of Drupal core and a collection of contributed modules and themes that work together to provide a more functional site for a specific purpose. Distributions are available at *http://drupal.org/ project/distributions* for e-commerce, government, non-profits, and many other purposes.

And finally, you can download translations for Drupal and its contributed modules, themes, and distributions from *http://localize.drupal.org*. As of Drupal version 7, this is unfortunately more complicated than installing a module or theme, even more so if you want to set up a multilingual site. It should be improved in Drupal 8.

Finding Drupal add-ons

Here are the main ways to find Drupal add-ons (modules, themes, or distributions):

- To find a specific add-on that you know the name of, visit *http://drupal.org* and type the name into the search box.

- If it's not in the first few results, try restricting the search to modules or themes, using the filters in the right sidebar (there is no way to restrict to distributions as of this writing).

- Alternatively, start by navigating to *http://drupal.org/project/modules*, *http:// drupal.org/project/themes*, or *http://drupal.org/project/distributions*, and searching from there.

- You can try guessing the URL, which is always *drupal.org/project/*, followed by the *machine name* of the project. The machine name is composed of lowercase letters, numbers, and underscores, but as the machine names are chosen by developers, some are hard to guess and they may take a couple of tries. For example, the Views module is at *http://drupal.org/project/views*; the Pixture Reloaded theme is at *http:// drupal.org/project/pixture_reloaded*; the XML Sitemap module is at *http:// drupal.org/project/xmlsitemap*.

- If you don't know the name, you can search from *http://drupal.org/project/modules*, *http://drupal.org/project/themes*, or *http://drupal.org/project/distributions* by keyword, Drupal version compatibility, or category (for modules only).

How Drupal Handles URL Requests

When Drupal is installed properly and the web server receives an HTTP request that corresponds to the Drupal site, the main Drupal *index.php* file is loaded and executed by the server to handle the request. It is important for Drupal programmers to understand how Drupal handles such requests; here is an overview (see also Figure 1-1):

1. Drupal determines which *settings.php* file to use for the HTTP request (you can set up Drupal to serve multiple sites, each with its own *settings.php* file), and this file is loaded and executed.

2. If a URL request is coming from an *anonymous user* (a site visitor who is not logged in), the *page cache* is checked to see if output has previously been cached for the same requested URL. If so, the cached output is returned to the web server, and Drupal is done. Drupal page caching does not apply to *authenticated* (logged-in) users.

3. The database connection, configuration/variable system, and PHP session variables are initialized.

4. The language system is initialized, and various files are loaded and executed (core include files and enabled modules' *.module* files).

5. Drupal determines whether the site is *offline* (also known as being in *maintenance mode*) or *online*.

6. If the site is offline, Drupal retrieves the offline message stored by an administrator as the page content. Other functions are called to generate some sections of the page content.

7. If the site is online, or if an authorized user is accessing a page while the site is offline, Drupal determines which functions need to be called to generate the content for the request, and calls these functions. They ideally return raw, prerendered content, but they could also return rendered or partially rendered content.

8. Drupal determines what *delivery method* to use for the page, and calls the appropriate delivery function.

9. For HTML page requests, the default page delivery function prints HTTP headers, uses the theme to render the raw content into HTML, prints the HTML output

(which effectively sends it to the web server), saves user session information to the database, and exits. The AJAX request delivery function is similar, but it renders into JSON output instead of using the theme system to render to HTML. Modules can also define custom page delivery methods.

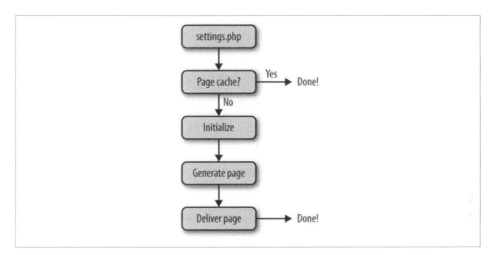

Figure 1-1. Overview of Drupal HTTP request handling

Related topics:

- "The Drupal Cache" (page 6)
- "Providing Page and Block Output" (page 55)
- "Where to Find More Information" (page vii) (web technology section—to find resources for learning about how web servers process requests in general)

Drupal 8

In Drupal 8, some of this high-level overview will still apply, although the details behind the steps will be changing significantly. In particular, fewer files will get loaded, and philosophically, Drupal will be oriented towards responding to generic HTTP requests containing session variables and other context information, rather than returning HTML pages given a URL.

The Drupal Cache

Drupal has a *cache* system, which allows modules to precalculate data or output and store it in the database so that the next time it is needed it doesn't have to be calculated again. This can save a lot of time on page loads, at the expense of some added complexity: any module that uses caching needs to take care to clear its cached data whenever the data is invalidated due to changes in dependent data. The Drupal 7 cache system has a fairly simple API, consisting of functions `cache_set()` and `cache_get()` (with a few variations), as well as `cache_clear_all()` to clear all database caches, including module-specific caches. Modules can register to have their caches cleared by implementing a *hook* (hooks are module entry points to altering Drupal) called `hook_flush_caches()`.

Both Drupal core and add-on modules cache information using this system. Here are a few examples:

- Page output for anonymous users (page caching can be turned off from the Performance configuration page)
- Block output (block caching can also be turned off from the Performance page)
- Menu routing (URL) information, block registration information, and other information collected from modules
- Theme information, including the list of theme regions and theme-related information from modules and themes
- Form arrays

Programmers and site builders new to Drupal quickly learn that the first thing to try, if they are having trouble with a site or if programming changes they have recently made are not being recognized, is to clear the cache. You can clear the cache by visiting the Performance configuration page and clicking the cache clear button, or by using Drush.

Related topics, examples, and references:

- See "Principle: Drupal Is Alterable" (page 9) to learn more about hooks in general, including theme hooks
- See *http://api.drupal.org* to find full documentation of the cache functions mentioned here
- For more information on Drush, see "Drupal Development Tools" (page 95)
- The Cache example from the Examples for Developers project (*http://drupal.org/project/examples*) illustrates how to use the Cache API
- Cache in menu routing: "Registering for a URL" (page 51) and the Page example from Examples for Developers

- Cache in block registration: "Registering a Block" (page 54) and the Block example from Examples for Developers

- Views cache: "Creating Views Module Add-Ons" (page 80)

- Theme cache: "Defining Theme Regions for Block Placement" (page 40) and "Making Your Output Themeable" (page 13)

- Forms: "Generating Forms with the Form API" (page 59) and the Form example from Examples for Developers

Drupal 8
The cache API functions are different in Drupal 8 because it uses classes to manage caching.

CHAPTER 2

Drupal Programming Principles

Experienced programmers learn, from training and experience, a set of principles and best practices to apply whenever they approach a problem they want to solve with programming. These include general practices such as "Comment your code" and "Choose clear variable names," which apply to all programming languages and situations, and some that are specific to a particular domain. Drupal has its own set of programming principles (covered in this chapter); learning them and following them should help you be a more effective Drupal programmer.

 If you are completely new to Drupal programming, you might find it useful to download the Examples for Developers project from *http:// drupal.org/project/examples* before reading this chapter. Try out the Page and Block examples, and take a look at their source code. Then come back and you'll have a little more context for learning these principles.

Principle: Drupal Is Alterable

Since Drupal is intended to be used as a platform for building web applications, one of its fundamental principles is that nearly everything about it needs to be customizable, and it needs to be customizable without having to edit its base source code. Since you're not supposed to need to edit the base code to build any type of web application with Drupal, both Drupal core and contributed modules are (ideally) fully *alterable*, meaning that they provide *hooks* that you can use to customize their behavior and output.

The term "hook" is used in a similar manner in several CMS projects, to mean an entry point where an add-on module or plugin can act to alter the behavior or output of the base CMS. In Drupal specifically, there are several somewhat overlapping types of hooks:

- Generic *hooks*, which allow modules to define additions to Drupal behavior.
- *Alter hooks*, which allow modules to make modifications to existing Drupal behavior.
- *Theme hooks*, which allow themes to modify the output that is sent to the browser.
- Theme hooks come with *theme preprocessing and processing hooks*, which modules can use to alter the information that is sent to the theme for output.

Why Not Just Hack (Edit) the Code?

Unlike in some other programming communities, the word "hack" in the Drupal community has definite negative connotations: hacking specifically means editing code that you downloaded from Drupal.org, in order to make a change that you need for a site. Hacking is highly discouraged; "hacking core," or editing the Drupal core files, is considered to be the worst offense. There are several reasons:

- Hacking is usually unnecessary, since there should be a hook available that will let you accomplish your goal without hacking.
- If you have hacked Drupal core or other downloaded code, updates will be much more difficult, because you will need to re-apply your hack after downloading a new version of the code. All downloaded code is at least occasionally updated with security fixes, bug fixes, and new features.
- If you program with hooks instead of hacking, you can turn off your changes by disabling the module containing the hooks. If you hack code, you will need to "unhack" it to turn off your changes.
- If you find that the hook you need does not exist, or if you are tempted to hack in order to fix a bug or add a new feature to a module, turn your hack into a patch and it becomes a benefit to you and the Drupal community if it is added to the module or to Drupal core.

Further reading:

- The "Hooks" topic on *http://api.drupal.org* lists all Drupal core generic and alter hooks, and the "Default theme implementations" topic lists all Drupal core theme hooks.
- Patches: "Reporting Issues and Contributing Code to the Drupal Community" (page 46)

Drupal 8

Drupal version 8 will certainly also be alterable, but it will use a combination of hooks and a new plugin system.

Programming with Hooks in Modules and Themes

Fundamentally (at least, from the point of view of a Drupal programmer and in versions up through Drupal 7), modules are mostly collections of hook *implementations* (PHP functions that define the hook's output or behavior), and themes are mostly collections of theme hook *overrides* (PHP functions or template files that define how output is presented); both themes and modules may also contain supporting code, CSS, JavaScript, images, and other files. When your objective is to alter Drupal, generally you should override theme hooks in a theme if your aim is to change the presentation of data, such as the exact HTML markup and CSS, and you should implement hooks in a module if your aim is to change the way Drupal behaves or what data is being output. If you need to do both, you will probably need to set up both a theme and a module.

To set up a module or theme and implement or override hooks, follow these steps:

1. Pick a *machine name* or *short name* for the module or theme. This is usually a sequence of letters and underscores, sometimes with numbers, that must follow PHP's function-naming conventions, since it will be used as a function prefix (use the machine name as a prefix for all functions you define in your module or theme). Pick a name that is not already in use by a project on drupal.org, to avoid later conflicts. Throughout this book, the convention is that you are creating a module called 'mymodule' or a theme called 'mytheme'.

2. Create a directory for your theme or module. See the "Where to Put Modules and Themes" (page 13) sidebar to figure out where to put this directory.

3. Create a file called *mymodule.info* or *mytheme.info* inside your directory, which is a plain text file that contains information about the module or theme. The exact syntax of this file tends to vary from version to version of Drupal and is slightly different for modules and themes, so check the online documentation, or copy a file from a module or theme provided in Drupal core or the Examples for Developers project to use as a starting point. Here's a minimal example for a Drupal 7 module (the syntax of this much is the same for themes):

```
; Comments start with a semicolon.
; The name displayed on the Modules or Themes list.
name = My Module
; The longer description displayed on the Modules or Themes list.
description = Longer description of this module.
; The Drupal core version this module or theme is compatible with.
core = 7.x
```

4. For theme and module hook functions, inside the same directory create a PHP file for your hook implementation or override functions (skip this step for theme templates). For theme hook functions, this file is called *template.php*. For most generic module hook functions, this file is called *mymodule.module*, but there are a few hook implementations that belong in other files. For instance, implementations of install-related hooks such as `hook_schema()` and `hook_update_N()` go into the *mymodule.install* file, and the contributed Views module uses two separate files for its hooks. Always read the reference documentation for the hook you are implementing to find out where its implementation belongs.

5. Within your module or theme file, define a function to implement the hook or override the theme function (skip this step for theme templates). For a hook called `hook_foo()`, the function must be named `mymodule_foo()`. For a theme hook function called `theme_foo()`, the function must be called `mytheme_foo()`. For the function body, often there is a good starting point in the hook documentation or the theme hook function you are overriding.

6. To override a theme hook template file, copy the template file you are overriding to your theme directory, keeping the same file name.

7. Edit the function or file to make the desired changes.

8. Enable your module or theme.

9. As you are programming and testing, if you add a new hook implementation or theme override to an enabled module or theme, you will need to clear the Drupal cache so that Drupal will recognize your change. For some informational hooks, you will also need to clear the cache when you make a change to the function body, to force Drupal to re-run your hook and read the new information. In general, it's always a good idea while you are developing to clear the cache after any change.

 There has been some discussion about changing the hook implementation function naming convention to `mymodule__foo()` (two underscores instead of one) for Drupal 8 or some later Drupal version, because many modules and many hooks have underscores in their names, and having a double underscore as the separator would make the distinction clearer. However, as of this writing, this has not yet been adopted.

Further reading, references, and examples:

- Documentation of .info file syntax for modules: *http://bit.ly/U0SuhH*
- Documentation of .info file syntax for themes: *http://bit.ly/Tol9P7*
- "The Drupal Cache" (page 6)

- Individual hook documentation can be found by searching for the hook function or template file name, such as hook_block_info, theme_table, or *block.tpl.php*, on *http://api.drupal.org*. Hook documentation pages give you documentation about the purpose of the hook, parameters, return value, which file the hook should be located in, a list of places where the hook is invoked (that is, which Drupal system will call your hook implementation function), and a list of other implementations in Drupal core. The function body for a hook function is a sample implementation. Theme hook pages tell you where the theme hook is used and document the variables you can use in your output.

- Database schema and installation hooks: "Setting Up Database Tables: Schema API and hook_update_N()" (page 22)

- Views hooks: "Creating Views Module Add-Ons" (page 80)

- Check if a proposed machine name for your module or theme is already in use by trying the URL *drupal.org/project/your_proposed_name*

Where to Put Modules and Themes

In Drupal 7 and earlier versions, modules and themes that you download or create should generally go into the *sites/all/modules* and *sites/all/themes* directories. Each module or theme project should be in its own subdirectory, such as *sites/all/modules/views* for the Views project. You can also organize modules into subdirectories; for example, you could create *sites/all/modules/contrib* and *sites/all/modules/custom* directories for downloaded ("contributed") modules and custom modules, respectively.

If you have a multisite installation and want a module or theme to be available to only one of the sites, you can put it in *sites/specific_site/modules* or *sites/specific_site/themes*. See *http://drupal.org/documentation/install/multi-site* for more information on this topic.

In Drupal 8, all of the Drupal core code (include files, modules, themes, and so on) has been moved to the directory *core*, and while you can still put your downloaded and custom modules into *sites/all*, there are also top-level *modules* and *themes* directories available. The use of these top-level directories is recommended, except for site-specific modules and themes in a multisite installation.

Making Your Output Themeable

Drupal's theme system is designed to separate the data and content from the styling and presentation: the module has control over the data and content, and the theme that is in use should have full control over styling and presentation, including rendering data into HTML. The basic principle that makes this work is that all data that is rendered into HTML should be passed through the Drupal theme() function. For instance, whenever a block from the core Block module is rendered, a call is made to theme('block', $block_data), rather than having the Block module simply output an HTML <div> containing the data. This allows your theme to override the default *block.tpl.php* theme template file, replacing the default <div> with different HTML if desired. The first argument to the theme() function is the theme hook name ('block' in this example), and the second argument is an array containing the data and attributes needed by the theme hook for rendering.

> **Theme functions versus render arrays**
> There is often confusion around the relationship between theme functions and *render arrays* (which are arrays containing the data to be output). The basic idea is that each element in a render array is *rendered* (converted into an HTML string) by a theme function or theme template, and rendering should be done as late as possible in the page-generating process. So, you should generally return render arrays from your functions that provide block and page output, and define theme functions or templates as needed (as described in this section), to render the elements of the output render arrays.

Modules that you write should follow the same principle: if your module outputs data as HTML, it should use the Drupal theme system to render the output instead of creating the HTML directly. Here is an outline of the steps; you might want to pull up the Theming example from Examples for Developers and follow along:

1. See if there is already a theme hook for the type of output you are generating. For instance, if you are generating an HTML table, you should use the Drupal core 'table' theme hook instead of defining your own hook.

2. If there is not already an appropriate theme hook, define a custom theme hook by implementing hook_theme() in your *mymodule.module* file. Example:

```
function mymodule_theme($existing, $type, $theme, $path) {
  return array(
    // The array keys are names of the theme hooks you are defining.
    'mymodule_hookname' => array(
      // Input variables.
      'variables' => array(
        // These are passed as an array to theme(), which passes them on
        // to your theme function or template. Here, provide default values.
        'input1' => '',
      ),
      // If you want to use a template, include this line; for a theme
      // function, leave it out.
```

```
            'template' => 'mymodule-hookname',
        ),
    );
}
```

3. Define a default implementation of your theme hook in your module. If your theme hook is named `'mymodule_hookname'`, this is either a theme function called `theme_mymymodule_hookname()`, or a theme template file called *mymodule-hookname.tpl.php*. Template files are generally preferred to theme functions. Template files should print the data in appropriate HTML markup; theme functions should compose a string containing the data and HTML markup and return that. For example:

```
// Sample theme function.
function theme_mymodule_hookname($variables) {
    return '<div>' . $variables['input1'] . '</div>';
}

// Same output as a theme template file.
<div><?php print $input1; ?></div>
```

4. If you are using a theme template, declare it in your *mymodule.info* file with a `files[] = mymodule-hookname.tpl.php` line.

5. Try to keep the programming in your theme function or template file to a minimum —it should just be putting the output inside some HTML markup. Any programming logic should instead be put into a function called `template_preprocess_mymodule_hookname()`, defined in your *mymodule.module* file. This function will automatically be called to preprocess the input data into the variables that can be printed by the template file.

6. Call `theme('mymodule_hookname', $data)` directly in your module to render the data. Or, create a render array that refers to your theme hook.

Further reading and example code:

- Overriding theme hooks and implementing generic hooks: "Programming with Hooks in Modules and Themes" (page 11)
- Render arrays: "Providing Page and Block Output" (page 55)
- The Theming example in Examples for Developers: *http://drupal.org/project/exam ples*
- The "Default theme implementations" topic on *http://api.drupal.org* lists all Drupal core theme functions and template files. Each theme function or template page lists "theme calls" (places in Drupal core that call `theme('hook_name')` to use that theme hook).

Drupal 8

In Drupal 8, theme template files will be using the Twig templating system, with Twig files like *block.html.twig* replacing PHP template files like *block.tpl.php* from previous versions of Drupal; theme functions will also be replaced by Twig files.

Principle: Drupal Is International

Drupal core and Drupal contributed modules and themes are ideally constructed so that their user interface elements use English by default, but can be translated into other languages. Less universally (but still ideally), modules and themes should also be constructed so that any user-entered text for settings or content can be translated. If both of these principles are followed:

- You can build an English-language site.
- You can build a site whose language is not English.
- You can build a multilingual site.
- You can use the translation mechanism to change the default English user interface text supplied by a module (for instance, changing the text on a button or link), without altering the module code.

When you program for Drupal, even if you don't think you will ever need to translate your site, it is still a good idea to follow this principle, because:

- The world is getting more global, and you might eventually need to translate your site.
- You might decide to contribute the module on drupal.org so that others can use it.
- It's a good Drupal coding habit to get into, in case you ever want to contribute code to the Drupal project.
- At least for built-in user interface text, it's not very difficult anyway.

Unicode strings

When programming with an international audience in mind, it is important to remember that not all text is ASCII—character sets for much of the world are instead multibyte Unicode characters. Some of the standard PHP string functions, such as `strlen()`, `strtolower()`, etc., do not take this into consideration and are not safe to use for multibyte characters. Instead, you can use Drupal's multibyte-safe equivalent functions (`drupal_strlen()`, and so on).

Internationalizing User Interface Text

The basic tool for internationalizing user interface text in the modules and themes you create is Drupal's t() function. Any text that will be shown to an administrative user or a site visitor should be enclosed in t(); before the text is printed, Drupal will translate it to the appropriate language. For instance:

```
// Bad:
$button_text = 'Save';
// Good:
$button_text = t('Save');
```

For translation to work properly, the first argument of t() must always be a literal string —it cannot contain variables. (This is because the first arguments to t() are extracted from code to build the database of strings that need translation.) If you need to substitute variable information into your string, t() has a mechanism:

```
// Bad:
$message_string = t("Hello $user_name");
// Good:
$message_string = t('Hello @user_name', array('@user_name' => $user_name));
```

As you can see, it doesn't really take much effort to make basic module-defined or theme-defined user interface text translatable. There are additional Drupal functions you can use to internationalize numbers, dates, and JavaScript text; these are collectively known as the Drupal Localization API. There is also a Drupal.t() function that is the equivalent to t() for use in JavaScript code, and an st() function for use in contexts where the full Drupal localization system is not available (such as during installation).

Further reading and references:

- Find Drupal localization functions on *http://api.drupal.org* listed in the "Formatting" and "Sanitization" topics.
- Read more about the Localization API at *http://drupal.org/developing/api/localiza tion*

Drupal 8
The t() function is not expected to change in Drupal 8.

Internationalizing User-Entered Text

If you are building a module that has user-entered settings or user-entered text that is then displayed to other users and you want your module to be fully internationalized so that it can be used on a multilingual site, you need to provide a way for the user-entered text to be translated. The t() function only works for literal text strings, so it cannot be used for this purpose.

Unfortunately, as of Drupal version 7, there is no Drupal core API for translating user-entered text in a uniform way. This situation will be remedied in Drupal version 8, since there is a major internationalization development effort underway (as of this writing). Meanwhile, in Drupal 7, if you do want your module's user-entered text to be internationalized and translatable, do one or more of the following:

- Store user-entered text in individual Drupal *variables*, using the variable_get() and variable_set() functions. If each string of user-entered text is stored in its own variable, and the variables are declared using the contributed Variable module's hook_variable_info(), site builders can use the contributed Internationalization module to translate this text. This is most appropriate if you just have a few administrator-entered text strings that need to be translated.

- For settings that form a list, use a Drupal core taxonomy vocabulary to manage the list instead of managing it in your own module. The taxonomy terms can then be translated using the contributed Internationalization module. To set up a vocabulary, you will need to add the following code to your module's hook_enable() implementation in the *mymodule.install* file:

```
// Create the vocabulary if it doesn't already exist.
$vocabulary = taxonomy_vocabulary_load(variable_get('mymodule_vocabulary', 0));
if (!$vocabulary) {
  $vocabulary = (object) array(
    'name' => t('Some appropriate name'),
    'machine_name' => 'mymodule_appropriate_name',
    'description' => t('Some appropriate description'),
    'module' => 'mymodule',
  );
  taxonomy_vocabulary_save($vocabulary);
  variable_set('mymodule_vocabulary', $vocabulary->vid);
}
```

- For more complicated collections of settings, define a Drupal *entity* with *fields* to store your settings. The collections of settings can then be translated using the Entity Translation module, which is expected to be added to Drupal core version 8.

Further reading and references:

- General information about programming with hooks: "Programming with Hooks in Modules and Themes" (page 11)
- Define an entity with fields: "Defining an Entity Type" (page 68)
- Internationalization module: *http://drupal.org/project/i18n*
- Variable module: *http://drupal.org/project/variable*
- Entity Translation module: *http://drupal.org/project/entity_translation*

Drupal 8

The `variable_get()` and `variable_set()` functions will be replaced in Drupal 8 with a new Configuration API, which will be internationalized in Drupal 8. The programming behind the taxonomy and entity systems will also be updated for Drupal 8 somewhat (more object-oriented), but the data storage and internationalization will be similar.

Principle: Drupal Is Accessible and Usable

The World Wide Web Consortium (W3C) defines *accessibility* as meaning that people with disabilities can perceive, understand, interact with, and contribute to a website, and their Web Accessibility Initiative (WAI) has many resources for learning about accessibility and testing websites for accessibility. The Drupal project has an active accessibility team, and one of Drupal's guiding principles is that its administrative backend and its visitor-facing output should both be as accessible as possible. The Drupal accessibility team has helped to improve the accessibility of Drupal by maintaining documentation on accessibility, testing Drupal for accessibility problems, and pushing the Drupal project to adopt industry-wide accessibility standards.

Another principle that ideally guides web design is *usability*: the idea that websites' user interfaces should be easy to use and learn. The Drupal project has an active usability team, and a commitment to high usability of the Drupal administrative interface is one of Drupal's guiding principles. The Drupal usability team has done usability studies and proposed changes that have greatly improved the usability of Drupal—there was a large usability push for Drupal version 7, and this is expected to continue through future versions of Drupal.

At times, usability and accessibility can be at odds. For instance, usability studies might show that a drag-and-drop interface for ordering menu items is much faster and more intuitive than an interface where you assign numerical weights to define the order, but blind users and users who have mobility limitations that preclude use of a mouse cannot use drag-and-drop interfaces, so the drag-and-drop interface has accessibility problems.

To satisfy both usability and accessibility principles, you can supply the drag-and-drop interface along with a link that lets users switch to the numerical weight interface if needed. Also, usability can sometimes be at odds with itself: for instance, an interface that provides more information when you hover your mouse over an area might be quite usable for someone using a mouse on a standard computer, but how do you "hover" on a mobile phone interface?

So, instead of thinking that usability and accessibility are incompatible, the guiding principle of combining usability and accessibility should be to make the user interface for a task as easy to use and learn as possible for users without mobility, sight, or other limitations, while providing alternatives that allow users with these limitations to be able to accomplish the task. In addition, when thinking about and testing for usability, different types of devices and browsers should be considered. Drupal aims to follow these principles, and you should also try to adopt them in your own programming. Here are some things you can do to improve accessibility and usability in your programming:

- Familiarize yourself with the usability and accessibility guidelines of the Drupal project.
- When providing a user interface in your own module, use the same user interface patterns as Drupal core (they have already been tested for usability and accessibility, and uniformity also means easier learning).
- When adding an administrative page for your module, put it in an appropriate section of the existing administrative user interface hierarchy of Drupal core, so people can find it easily.
- Test your user interfaces and theme for accessibility.
- Make sure that all information you present is available in text format (not just in images or diagrams), so screen reader users can access it. Search engines also only index text information, so making your site accessible in this way will also help its visibility in search engines.
- Make your theme and user interface designs adaptable to different screen sizes and magnifications. This will help with both usability on mobile devices and accessibility for people who need to magnify their screens.

Further reading and references:

- World Wide Web Consortium (W3C): *http://w3.org*
- Web Accessibility Initiative (WAI)—includes resources for accessibility testing and world wide standards: *http://www.w3.org/WAI/*
- Drupal accessibility team: *http://groups.drupal.org/accessibility*
- Drupal accessibility guidelines and resources: *http://drupal.org/about/accessibility*
- Drupal usability team: *http://groups.drupal.org/usability*

- Drupal usability guidelines: *http://drupal.org/ui-standards*

Principle: Drupal Is Database Independent

Although most Drupal sites use MySQL (or a compatible clone) as the database backend, Drupal version 7 (and later versions) can be used with a variety of databases: Drupal core supports PostgreSQL and SQLite, and contributed modules add support for other databases. Drupal core also provides several database-related customizations, such as the ability to prefix database table names with a string, or different strings for different tables, and to fall back to a different database if the default database is not available. In order to facilitate this portability, Drupal provides a Schema API and a Database API, which work together as a framework for defining and querying database tables.

Since Drupal is written in PHP, it is possible in your own programming to avoid using the Drupal Schema and Database APIs and instead use the PHP database functions you may be familiar with to query the database directly. But this is not a good idea, because:

- Using the Database API helps make your queries more secure from SQL injection bugs.
- The Schema API is actually easier to use for creating and modifying tables than writing your own SQL queries, and the code is easier to read and maintain. The Database API takes an effort similar to writing your own SQL queries.
- You might sometime want to switch to a different database for performance reasons.
- You might sometime want to use different site set-up choices, such as setting up development and staging sites with different database options.
- You might want to contribute your module on drupal.org so that others can use it.
- It's a good habit to get into, in case you ever want to contribute code to the Drupal project.

It should be noted that one of the best ways to make sure to stay independent of the database is to avoid direct use of the database entirely. For instance, instead of creating a module to store information in its own custom database table, consider whether you can use Drupal's taxonomy, node, or entity system instead. Or perhaps you can use a contributed module, along with a custom plugin.

Further reading and references:

- The rest of this section has more details on the Database and Schema APIs.
- Avoiding database programming entirely: "Mistake: Programming Too Much" (page 35)
- Security concerns: "Principle: Drupal Is Secure; User Input Is Insecure" (page 27)

- Drupal Schema API: *http://drupal.org/developing/api/schema*
- Drupal Database API: *http://drupal.org/developing/api/database*
- Modules providing alternative database integration: MongoDB (*http://drupal.org/project/mongodb*), Microsoft SQL Server (*http://drupal.org/project/sqlsrv*), Oracle (*http://drupal.org/project/oracle*)
- Group for people interested in enterprise applications (including database integration): *http://groups.drupal.org/enterprise*

Drupal 8

The Database and Schema APIs are not expected to change significantly in Drupal 8, except that the PHP classes that the Database API uses are namespaced in Drupal 8, are found in different files, and may have slightly different names in the Drupal source code. This should not significantly affect programming with databases.

Setting Up Database Tables: Schema API and hook_update_N()

If your module really does need to set up its own database tables, create them by implementing hook_schema() in your *mymodule.install* file. Drupal will then take care of creating the tables when your module is enabled, as well as deleting them when your module is uninstalled. For example, to define a database table called 'mymodule_foo' with fields 'bar' and 'baz':

```
function mymodule_schema() {
  $schema = array();
  $schema['mymodule_foo'] = array(
    'description' => 'Untranslated description of this table',
    'fields' => array(
      'bar' => array(
        'description' => 'Untranslated description of this field',
        'type' => 'varchar',
        'length' => 50,
        'default' => '',
      ),
      'baz' => array(
        'description' => 'Untranslated description of this field',
        'type' => 'int',
        'unsigned' => TRUE,
        'default' => 0,
      ),
    ),
    'primary key' => array('baz'),
  );
  return $schema;
}
```

The Schema API is flexible enough to define all aspects of database tables, including fields of different types, indexes, and so on. See the Schema API documentation for details.

Once you have enabled a module and its database tables are created, you may find that you need to make a change, such as adding a field, deleting a field, adding a new database table, and so on, to correspond to a new feature you have added to your module. The Schema API provides a standard way to do this:

1. Add a hook_update_N() implementation (also known as an *update function*) to your *mymodule.install* file, which will update the database using functions such as db_add_field(), db_create_table(), etc. Update functions are named sequentially, and each builds upon the previous schema and updates. The comment directly before the function is shown on the Pending Updates page when you run the *example.com/update.php* script, so make this comment coherent and descriptive. For example, this function would change the length of the 'bar' field to 150 characters, and also add a new field 'bay':

```
/**
 * Make one field wider and add a new field in the mymodule_foo table.
 */
function mymodule_update_7001() {
  db_change_field('mymodule_foo', 'bar', 'bar', array(
    'description' => 'Untranslated description of this field',
    'type' => 'varchar',
    'length' => 150,
    'default' => '',
  ));
  db_add_field('mymodule_foo', 'bay', array(
    'description' => 'Untranslated description of this field',
    'type' => 'varchar',
    'length' => 50,
    'default' => '',
  ));
}
```

2. Edit your original hook_schema() implementation function, making corresponding changes to the schema.

3. Make changes in your module code to use the new schema.

4. If this is for a site you manage, run the update script by visiting *example.com/ update.php*. You will be presented with a list of pending updates, which should include the update function you just created and show the description from the function comment.

Do not attempt to call Drupal Database API functions such as `dru pal_write_record()` that rely on the schema from an update function, because the schema will be in an unknown state while the update function is running.

Correspondingly, never reference your `hook_schema()` implementation in an update function—always write out the full array values in your calls to `db_change_field()` and similar functions. The reason is that if you ever decide to share your module with someone else, you will not have control over when the updates are run, so you don't know at the moment of running a particular update function what the state of the schema in `hook_schema()` might be.

Further reading, examples, and references:

- General information about programming with hooks: "Programming with Hooks in Modules and Themes" (page 11)
- Drupal Schema API: *http://drupal.org/developing/api/schema*
- The DBTNG example from Examples for Developers: *http://drupal.org/project/ examples* (DBTNG is the nickname for the Database API that originated in Drupal 7, and stands for "Database: The Next Generation")
- Look up `hook_schema` and `hook_update_N` on *http://api.drupal.org* for full details of their return values.
- The functions that update database tables, such as `db_change_field()`, can be found in the *database.inc* include file (at least in Drupal 7). You can look this file up on *http://api.drupal.org* to find a list of all its functions.

Querying the Database with the Database API

If your module needs to query the Drupal database directly, whether querying its own tables or tables provided by Drupal core or another module, you will need to use the Drupal Database API to ensure that your queries are secure and portable. The Database API provides the `db_query()` function, which you can use to make simple queries, and a dynamic API that can be used for arbitrarily complex queries.

Very simple queries

For the simplest SELECT queries, you can use the Drupal `db_query()` function:

```
$result = db_query('SELECT * FROM {users} u WHERE u.status = :status',
  array(':status' => $desired_status));
foreach ($result as $record) {
```

```
    // $record will be a PHP object with fields corresponding to the table fields.
    $user_name = $record->name;
    // ...
}
```

Notes:

- The name of the database table being queried must be enclosed in {}. When Drupal runs the query, this table name will be prefixed as necessary.

- Variable inputs to the query use *placeholders*, which start with : and should contain only letters (numbers, underscores, and so on will not work in all cases). The second argument to db_query() is an array giving the values of the placeholders. Never put variable inputs directly into your query strings, especially if they originate in insecure user input.

- If a placeholder is a string, do not enclose it in quotes in the query—the variable substitution will take care of adding the quotes as necessary. For instance:

```
// Bad:
"WHERE u.name = ':name'"
// Good:
"WHERE u.name = :name"
```

- Only use db_query() for SELECT queries on a single database table, and only if SQL functions such as LIKE and grouping are not involved. The reason is that insert queries, delete queries, update queries, table joins, grouping, and some SQL functions are different across database engines, so to ensure portability, you will need to use the dynamic query Database API functions for these queries.

- Some Drupal database tables have permission implications (for instance, the Node module has a rich permission system for restricting access to certain content by certain users or roles). When querying such tables, do not use db_query(), because the query will need to be modified by Drupal to enforce the correct permissions. Use the dynamic query Database API functions instead.

- Drupal also has a built-in pager system that greatly simplifies making multiple-page queries. You will need to use the dynamic query functions to use this system.

Dynamic queries

For queries that involve more than one database table, paging, SQL functions such as LIKE, grouping, tables with access restrictions, or anything other than a SELECT, you will need to use Drupal's dynamic query functions instead of the simple db_query() function. These functions allow you to build up a query in a database-independent way, and then execute it to get the same type of result set returned by db_query().

For example:

```
// Equivalent to:
//   SELECT title, nid, created FROM {node} n WHERE n.status = 1
// with node access enforced.
$result = db_select('node', 'n')
  ->addTag('node_access') // Enforce node access permissions.
  ->fields('n', array('title', 'nid', 'created')) // Fields to return.
  ->condition('n.status', 1) // WHERE condition.
  ->execute();
foreach ($result as $node) {
  // $node will be a PHP object with fields corresponding to the table fields.
  $title = $node->title;
  // ...
}
```

Notes:

- Unlike when using the simple db_query(), do not enclose table names in {}.

- The addTag() method is used when you are querying a table with permissions considerations. For instance, the Node module has a complex permissions system, which is enforced for you in database queries if you add the 'node_access' tag to your query.

- Some query methods allow *chaining*, as illustrated in the previous example, because they alter the query in place and return the altered query object. Some do not; notably addField() and the join methods. If you use a non-chaining method, use syntax like this:

```
// Equivalent to:
//   SELECT n.changed AS last_updated, n.title, n.nid, u.name FROM
//   {node} n INNER JOIN {users} u ON u.uid = n.nid WHERE
//   n.status = 1
// with a pager, 20 items per page, and node access enforced.
$query = db_select('node', 'n');
$query->addField('n', 'changed', 'last_updated'); // Field with an alias.
$query->innerJoin('users', 'u', 'u.uid = n.uid'); // Join.
$query = $query->extend('PagerDefault'); // Paging.
$result = $query
  ->fields('n', array('title', 'nid'))
  ->fields('u', array('name'))
  ->addTag('node_access')
  ->condition('n.status', 1)
  ->limit(20) // Number of items per page.
  ->execute();
```

- When using a PagerDefault query, as in the previous example, add a standard pager to your output by calling theme('pager'). This will let Drupal handle all the details of getting the right items on each page.

Further reading, examples, and references:

- Avoiding database programming entirely: "Mistake: Programming Too Much" (page 35)
- Security concerns: "Principle: Drupal Is Secure; User Input Is Insecure" (page 27)
- Paged queries and output: "Generating paged output" (page 57)
- Drupal Database API: *http://drupal.org/developing/api/database*
- The DBTNG example from Examples for Developers: *http://drupal.org/project/ examples* (DBTNG is the nickname for the Database API that originated in Drupal 7, and stands for "Database: The Next Generation")
- The database query functions, such as db_select(), can be found in the *database.inc* include file (at least in Drupal 7). You can look this file up on *http:// api.drupal.org* to find a list of all its functions.

Principle: Drupal Is Secure; User Input Is Insecure

When programming for the web, you always need to think about security. The basic principle to follow is to consider all user-provided input to be insecure, whether it is provided by a trusted user such as a site administrator (who could be the target of hacking), a semi-trusted user such as someone with a generic user account on your site, or an anonymous site visitor. With that in mind, whatever you do in your Drupal programming that involves user-provided input, that input will first need to be cleansed or checked in some way to make it more secure.

Besides this basic principle, which applies to all web programming, Drupal has an additional security concern: your programming needs to respect Drupal's permission system. For instance, although a module you write can run arbitrary database queries, only information from the database that a particular user has permission to view should be shown to them. And although a module you write can technically call any Drupal API function at any time, you should not call functions without checking that the user has permission to perform their actions.

Both Drupal core and Drupal's contributed modules and themes ideally follow these principles of cleansing user input and checking Drupal permissions: the Drupal project has a volunteer security team, which handles reports of security violations, and every contributor's first module or theme is reviewed before it is allowed to be promoted to "full project" status on drupal.org. Your Drupal programming should also follow these principles, and the following sections will give you an introduction to making your Drupal code more secure. You will also need to make sure your site permissions are reasonable and take other measures to set up a secure site.

Further reading and resources:

- Securing a Drupal site: *http://drupal.org/security/secure-configuration*
- The Drupal site building section of "Where to Find More Information" (page vii) lists additional resources
- "Mistake: Saving PHP Code in the Database" (page 43)

Cleansing and Checking User-Provided Input

The philosophy used in Drupal for ensuring security with user-provided input is to store whatever the user typed in the database without alteration, and then cleanse it prior to display. Both of these steps must be done carefully.

In the database storage step, you need to be concerned about *SQL injection* attacks— malicious users could attempt to provide input that would, for instance, end the query you were using to add the data to the database, and run a query of their choice. If you use the Drupal database API correctly, however, all user-provided input will either be put into the query using placeholders or as arguments to safe methods such as condition(), and the integrity of your database will be protected.

In the output step, the Drupal API provides functions you can use to cleanse data to make it safe for HTML output. For instance, if you are outputting data that is supposed to be plain text (without HTML tags), you should pass it through the check_plain() function. If you are outputting data that is supposed to contain HTML tags (which should be limited for untrusted users), you should pass it through the check_markup() function. If you are outputting a user-provided URL, you should pass it through check_url(). However, note that some Drupal API functions, such as l() (for making links), cleanse input themselves, so read the function documentation and don't double-cleanse. Examples:

```
// Bad:
print '<p>' . $text . '</p>';
print '<a href="' . $url . '">' . $text . '</a>';
print l(check_plain($text), check_url($url));
// Good:
print '<p>' . check_plain($text) . '</p>';
print l($text, $url);
```

Further reading, examples, and references:

- Drupal database API: "Querying the Database with the Database API" (page 24)
- Drupal functions that cleanse data can be found on *http://api.drupal.org* under the "Sanitization" topic.
- More about writing secure code: *http://drupal.org/writing-secure-code*

- "Mistake: Saving PHP Code in the Database" (page 43)

Checking Drupal Permissions

Drupal has a rich permission system, which your modules need to interact with properly to ensure that users, including anonymous site visitors, are only allowed to see information and perform actions that they have permission for. There are several systems for permissions checking in Drupal core, and some contributed modules have their own permissions systems. It is important to understand the permissions systems of all modules that your module interacts with.

Drupal core's main permission system

The main system for permissions checking in Drupal core works as follows:

- Modules define permissions by implementing hook_permission() in their *mymodule.module* file

```
function mymodule_permission() {
  return array(
    // The array keys are the permissions' internal names.
    'administer mymodule' => array(
      'title' => t('Administer My Module settings'), // Human-readable name.
      'description' => t('Longer description only if it is really necessary.'),
    ),
    // Define additional permissions by adding more array elements.
  );
}
```

- In the Drupal user interface, site administrators can define *roles*, and grant one or more permissions to each role. A user account can then be assigned to one or more roles, which grants all of the roles' permissions to that user account.

- When a module performs an action on behalf of a user, or displays information to the user, it calls user_access('internal permission name') to see whether the current user has the needed permission, and only performs the action or displays the data if that is the case.

In your module programming, you need to be aware of permissions that other modules define, and make sure to call user_access() as appropriate when using that module's functions. You also need to determine which actions your module defines that should be restricted, define appropriate permissions for them, and use user_access() to verify the permissions.

Luckily, in some cases Drupal will check permissions for you, which makes this system pretty easy to use. For instance, when you are defining menu routing URLs with hook_menu(), you define permissions for that URL, and Drupal enforces the permissions by calling the designated access callback function, which defaults to user_access().

Further reading, examples, and references:

- General information about programming with hooks: "Programming with Hooks in Modules and Themes" (page 11)
- URL registration permissions: "Registering for a URL" (page 51)
- Several of the examples from the Examples for Developers project (*http:// drupal.org/project/examples*) create or check permissions, such as the Cache example, the Tokens example, and the Menu example.

Permissions and security in forms

The Drupal Form API also has a permission and security system that you can take advantage of. This consists of the following components:

- When you are defining a form array, each form element can be given a Boolean '#access' property—TRUE means the form element is displayed and usable, and FALSE means it is not accessible to the current user. When you are building a form, you can assign the result of a user_access() call to the '#access' property of an element, to programmatically show/hide form elements.
- Assuming that you use the standard Drupal form functions to display and process the form, Drupal will protect against cross-site forgery form submissions by adding a unique token to the form and validating the token when the form is submitted. URL access permission will also be checked for the form submission URL.
- You should also use *confirmation forms* to prevent hacking attacks that might trick an administrative user into visiting a URL that would maliciously destroy or alter data. For instance, if your module has a URL that triggers deleting a particular database record, have that URL instead display a confirmation form, and only delete the database record if the action is confirmed.

Further reading, examples, and references:

- Defining a form array: "Generating Forms with the Form API" (page 59)
- Confirmation forms: "Using confirmation forms" (page 61)
- The Form example from Examples for Developers (*http://drupal.org/project/exam ples*)

Permissions in displaying and operating on content

Some Drupal core modules that manage content have complex permissions systems that also need to be considered in your module programming. For instance, the core Node module provides hooks that allow other modules to define permission systems for node content, which can be as simple as "Only allow users of role A to view node content of type B," or as complex as allowing access to particular node content items only to certain individual users. If you are writing a module that allows users to operate or view node content, you need to respect whatever permissions other modules may have defined. Similarly, if you are writing a module that deals with core taxonomy terms, comments, or content managed by a contributed module, you need to make sure that your module is complying with the content permission scheme that applies.

Luckily, modules that define complex content permissions have APIs that make obeying the permissions feasible, without knowing the details of the permissions that are in place on a particular site. For example, if you are writing a module that operates on individual node content items, you need to check access permissions by calling the `node_access()` function, passing in the operation you are performing (`'view'`, `'delete'`, etc.) and the node content item you are operating on. And if you are writing a module that queries the database to make a node content item listing, such as a block that lists content satisfying some criteria, you need to add the `node_access` tag to your database query. This will ensure that only items the user has permission to view are returned by the query, without having to guess at what particular permissions modules might be in use.

Further reading, examples, and references:

- "Programming with Entities and Fields" (page 66)
- Adding tags to queries: "Dynamic queries" (page 25)
- "Avoiding Custom Programming with Fielded Data" (page 39)
- The Node Access and Entity examples in the Examples for Developers project (*http://drupal.org/project/examples*)

Principle: Drupal Code Is Tested and Documented

There was a large effort during the Drupal version 7 development cycle to adopt the "Simpletest" automated testing framework for Drupal core, and to adhere to the development principle that all major functionality should have automated tests. A team within the Drupal project maintains a group of servers to run automated tests, and before any proposed change is committed to the Drupal core source code, all of the existing automated tests must pass (and if it proposes new functionality, a change must usually be accompanied by new tests to ensure that it works as expected). Many contributed module projects on drupal.org have also adopted this principle, at least to some extent.

A related effort in the Drupal project has been to improve the documentation of the code in Drupal core. The project has standards for in-code documentation, which include the idea that each function, class, file, and constant should include a documentation header (these documentation headers are parsed to create the Drupal API reference site). Most of the Drupal 7 code is reasonably well documented, and for the Drupal 8 development cycle, a standard was adopted to say that no change should be committed without its accompanying documentation being complete.

Adopting the "everything should be tested" and "everything should be documented" principles in your own programming is an excellent idea. Writing formal documentation headers before you start work on the code for a function or class is a great way to ensure that you've thought out what the function or class should do, and it will also help you or the next maintainer of the code to remember what the code was supposed to do. In addition, while writing tests for the functionality of your code does take time (and the testing framework takes some time to learn how to use), I have found that even basic tests usually find bugs in code that I would not otherwise be aware of, and having tests also greatly lessens the chance that feature additions or bug fixes added later will break existing functionality. Tests can also be considered to be another form of documentation, since they document the expected functionality of your code by testing that it performs the way it should. The Simpletest testing framework allows you to create both *unit tests* (low-level tests of specific functions or classes) and *functional tests* (higher-level tests that can involve simulating a browser and checking that pages and forms behave as they should); both can be appropriate for code that you write.

Resources and examples for testing and documentation:

- How to write and run automated tests: *http://drupal.org/simpletest*
- All of the examples in the Examples for Developers project (*http://drupal.org/project/examples*) have tests, and there are also many tests in Drupal core. In Drupal version 7, these files have extension *.test*, and they are located in the core module directories *modules/module_name*. In Drupal version 8, each test class is in its own *.php* file, and they are located in *core/modules/module_name/lib/Drupal/module_name/Tests/* directories. Contributed modules with tests either follow the same conventions, or in Drupal 7, may put the tests in a sub-directory *tests*.
- If you want to write tests for the Drupal project, look for issues tagged "needs tests" in a project that interests you (Drupal core or a contributed project).
- Module that parses API documentation for *http://api.drupal.org* (you can use it to build your own API documentation site): *http://drupal.org/project/api*
- Documentation standards: *http://drupal.org/coding-standards/docs*

- The Drupal core files for Drupal 7 and 8 are mostly pretty well documented and mostly adhere to the Drupal documentation standards.
- If you want to contribute API documentation to the Drupal project, look for issues in the "documentation" component in a project that interests you.

CHAPTER 3

Common Drupal Programming Mistakes

Experienced programmers have accumulated, through training or the experience of trial and error, a body of knowledge about how to approach problems and build applications. Unfortunately, some of this knowledge may lead them to make mistakes when they start working with Drupal, or to do things in less than optimal ways. This chapter covers several (somewhat overlapping) areas where programmers can shift their thinking or their approach in order to become more efficient at using the strengths of the Drupal platform, rather than fighting against it. Of course, following the principles in Chapter 2 will also help you shift your thinking to the Drupal way of doing things, and the suggestions and tools in Chapter 5 can help you avoid mistakes and find the mistakes that you do make.

Mistake: Programming Too Much

Experienced programmers who are new to Drupal often suffer from a variety of the "if all you have is a hammer, everything looks like a nail" syndrome: when faced with a challenge on a website (such as adding a feature or fixing a problem), they always try to solve it with programming. But although Drupal is built on PHP, and you can definitely do a lot of PHP programming when setting up a Drupal site, this is usually not the best approach: it results in a lot of unnecessary (and often tedious) programming. Related to this, experienced programmers coming to Drupal can be in a rush to become Drupal *programmers*, when really it would be better if they started out by becoming more effective Drupal *users* first, and resorted to programming only when necessary. While this goes against all the "solve all problems by programming" instincts of an experienced programmer (at least, speaking from my experience), if you learn advanced Drupal site building techniques before you dive into Drupal programming, you will reap many benefits:

- You will be in a position to create very complex and interesting websites with Drupal because of your strong site-building skills.

- You'll be doing more interesting programming tasks rather than tedious ones.

- You'll save time by taking advantage of previous efforts by others.

- You can use code that has been reviewed for security problems and tested on many other sites instead of custom code that is for only your site.

- You can take advantage of the internationalization and translation capabilities of built-in Drupal systems.

Here are some examples of Drupal site building knowledge you should explore in order to avoid unnecessary and tedious programming:

Customizing fielded content display

The core Fields administrative interface provides a lot of flexibility in defining how fields are displayed in content, including the order of fields, label placement, data formatting, and which fields are shown. If that is not enough, the Display Suite module can be helpful as can the Panels module.

Altering other user interface text

Drupal provides hooks that let you write a module that can alter page content and form elements. These can be quite useful, but often all you really need to do is change some text on a button or a form field label. If so, you don't need to program—use the String Overrides module. If you need to do something to a form beyond what String Overrides covers, you can alter a form in a module.

Content permissions

The Drupal core Node module allows add-on modules to define very flexible content access permissions. So, if you need something beyond the default Node module permissions, your first instinct might be to write a content access module. However, the permissions needed for most sites are covered by the contributed Content Access module, which allows you to define permissions on a per-content-type or per-content-item basis, which can be applied by role or by managing lists of individual users (with the addition of the Access Control Lists (ACL) module). If you do need a permission system that is more customized than what Content Access and other contributed content access modules provide, you will need to create a custom module.

Marking and classifying content

If your site needs content classification, use the core Taxonomy module rather than writing custom code. If users need to mark content (as bookmarked, spam, etc.), the contributed Flag module is the usual choice. There are also voting modules, such as Fivestar, if this is a feature you need on your site.

Placing content on pages

Rather than using PHP code or embedding content directly into custom theme template files or theme functions, use the Drupal core block system to place content into regions on pages. If your theme doesn't have a region that would allow you to put the content where you want it, add a region to your theme. If the block system is not flexible enough, the contributed Context module provides much more flexibility (it lets you define conditions that will display certain blocks to certain users on certain pages; if it does not completely cover your needs, it is also possible to create add-ons to provide more conditions and responses. Some people prefer to build page layouts with the contributed Panels module rather than using Context. Also note that the page layout and context system will be totally overhauled in Drupal 8.

Web forms

The contributed Webform module covers many web form use cases, and you can also learn its API and do a little programming if you need a form field type that is not included (but check to see if someone has already contributed a module that defines the form field that you need).

Responding to events

The contributed Rules module allows you to define responses (such as sending email or redirecting to a different page) to various events (such as updating or adding content) on your website, under certain conditions (such as matching a content type or user role). If the events, conditions, or responses defined by the Rules module do not cover your needs, you can extend it. The Notifications module can also be useful—it lets users subscribe to content updates on a site.

Site navigation

Novice Drupal programmers sometimes want to hardcode site navigation into their theme templates, because they have used this approach to ensure uniform navigation on custom-built PHP/MySQL or pure HTML sites in the past. While this is certainly possible, it's much better to use the core Menu module to manage site navigation. If you use the Menu module, you can define different *menus* for the main header navigation, the footer, sidebars, etc., and use CSS to style them appropriately. Drupal will automatically omit navigation items that are not accessible to whoever is viewing the site, and you will be able to manage the menus in the administrative user interface. If you hardcode them into a theme template file, they will be much more difficult to manage, and permissions will not be enforced.

Breadcrumbs

The default Drupal breadcrumbs for content pages are often not what is desired for a site. So, it is tempting to override them by programming. While that is sometimes necessary, many use cases are covered by the contributed Custom Breadcrumbs module, which is quite easy to set up.

Site configuration export

The contributed Features module lets you export much of the configuration of a Drupal site to PHP code. For instance, you can export your custom content types and fields, your Views, and many other settings; the result is a module, which you can then put into revision control or share with another site. However, note that not all contributed modules support Features export, so not all of your settings can be exported.

Further reading and examples:

- "Avoiding Custom Programming with Fielded Data" (page 39) (just below)
- "Defining Theme Regions for Block Placement" (page 40) (later in this section)
- Internationalization capabilities of Drupal: "Principle: Drupal Is International" (page 16)
- The Node Access example in Examples for Developers: *http://drupal.org/project/examples*
- "Creating Rules Module Add-Ons" (page 90)
- "Altering forms" (page 63)

Contributed modules mentioned in this section:

- Access Control Lists: *http://drupal.org/project/acl*
- Content Access: *http://drupal.org/project/content_access*
- Context: *http://drupal.org/project/context*
- Custom Breadcrumbs: *http://drupal.org/project/custom_breadcrumbs*
- Display Suite: *http://drupal.org/project/ds*
- Features: *http://drupal.org/project/features*
- Fivestar: *http://drupal.org/project/fivestar*
- Flag: *http://drupal.org/project/flag*
- Notifications: *http://drupal.org/project/notifications*
- Panels: *http://drupal.org/project/panels*
- Rules: *http://drupal.org/project/rules*
- String Overrides: *http://drupal.org/project/stringoverrides*
- Webform: *http://drupal.org/project/webform*

Avoiding Custom Programming with Fielded Data

While your first instinct, if you need to manage some fielded data on your website, might be to set up a custom database table to store your data, and to display your data using custom queries, you can save yourself a lot of unnecessary programming by instead using *entities*, fields, and the Views module. Entities are a new concept for Drupal version 7: modules define entity types to store information for a website, and the field system allows many different types of data to be attached to the base entity. Drupal core modules define four basic entity types (node content items, comments, taxonomy terms, and user accounts), and both Drupal core and contributed modules define fields to store various types of data (text, numbers, images, and so on).

So, rather than defining a database table in a custom module to store the custom data for your website, your first step should usually be to instead set up a custom node content type and add the fields you need to it. If your data is not semantically "content", you might be better off setting up a taxonomy vocabulary, or if it has very different properties from the core modules' concepts of content items, comments, taxonomy terms, or user accounts, you can create your own entity type (this will involve some programming).

Once you have your core or custom entity type set up with its fields, you should not need to do any more programming to query and display the data. Instead, use the Views module, which is basically a very flexible content query and display engine (you may also find the contributed Nodequeue module useful if you are using the node content entity for your data). Examples of pages, blocks, and feeds you can build with Views include:

- A photo gallery, which could allow searching by keyword, topic- or user-based galleries, and a block that displays a random image added within the past 24 hours.
- A "recent site updates" block.
- A News block that detects which section of the site it is being displayed on, and chooses news related to that site.
- A map of a company's offices, or of the site's registered users.
- Site archives with searching and filtering capability.

The way that Views works is that its user interface lets you set up the parameters for what is basically a formatted list of content (known as a "View"); these parameters can then be saved to PHP code if desired. This might not sound very exciting or useful, but when you come to understand that "lists" encompasses grids, clouds, tables, feeds, and other formats; and "content" encompasses node content items, taxonomy terms, files, user account data, and other Drupal entities, you will begin to see how flexible and powerful this module is. Then when you learn how to make *relationships* (basically query table joins) between content types, and how to use static, exposed, and contextual filters to define which content items are shown, you will really become a power Views user. Finally, you can even extend Views by creating custom output formats, data types, fields, and relationships, if the base module and available contributed Views add-on modules do not cover your use case.

So, rather than writing modules to define database tables and using custom database queries to create content lists or displays, instead define content types (or other entities), add fields to them, become a power Views user, and extend Views if you need to. There is help within the Views module itself that explains the basics (and some of the complexities), if you also install the Advanced Help module, and countless blog articles, video tutorials, and books covering the subject.

Further reading and references:

- "Programming with Entities and Fields" (page 66)
- "Creating Views Module Add-Ons" (page 80)
- Advanced Help module: *http://drupal.org/project/advanced_help*
- Nodequeue module: *http://drupal.org/project/nodequeue*
- Views module: *http://drupal.org/project/views*

Drupal 8
The Views module has been incorporated into Drupal core for version 8, and as of this writing, there is an effort underway to update many of the Drupal core pages that list content to use Views instead of custom queries.

Defining Theme Regions for Block Placement

Blocks in Drupal are placed in *regions* in your theme, which might include the header, footer, left sidebar, right sidebar, and main content region. In most themes, the regions are the same on every page, although the Drupal theme system allows you to define multiple templates, each containing different regions. Drupal core's block system allows you to place each block into a particular region, and then define conditions for whether the block should be visible or not on particular pages or for particular users. For some sites, this limited flexibility is not enough, so the contributed Context module or Panels module can be used to gain more flexibility in block placement.

Sometimes all you need to achieve your desired site layout is a new theme region to put blocks in. For instance, maybe your site design calls for a "Call to Action" section on some pages, which would have a contrasting color scheme and appear in the upper-right corner of the main content area of the page. You can use the Drupal core block system to control what appears there on each page, if you add a new region to your theme. Here are the steps:

1. If you are using a Drupal core theme or a theme you downloaded, start by making a custom *sub-theme*. This will let you inherit most of the base theme, while overriding just the parts that you want to change.

2. Add a line like the one below to the *mytheme.info* file, to tell Drupal about the new region. You will need to give the region both an internal name and a human-readable name for the Blocks administration page:

   ```
   regions[internal_region_name] = Readable region name
   ```

3. Add HTML to the *page.tpl.php* template file, or a specific template file like *page--front.tpl.php*, and CSS if necessary, to display the region's blocks or other content:

   ```
   <div id="internal-region-name">
     <?php print render($page['internal_region_name']); ?>
   </div>
   ```

4. Clear the Drupal cache, so that Drupal will recognize your new region.

Further reading and references:

- Creating a sub-theme: *http://bit.ly/TiVYNH*
- Drupal's theme system incorporates a process of automatic template overrides. For instance, if the site's home page is being displayed and your theme has a file called *page--front.php*, it will be used in place of the *page.tpl.php* template used for other pages. This process is called "Template Suggestions," and it is described in more detail on *http://bit.ly/SaQPsf*
- "The Drupal Cache" (page 6)

Drupal 8

The system for defining page regions described here will be different in Drupal 8. In Drupal 7 and prior versions, the theme or theme engine chooses which page template file to use for different pages on the site, while in Drupal 8, this will be governed by the new layouts system. Also, Drupal 8 will be using the Twig template system in place of PHP template files.

Mistake: Misusing the Drupal API

Drupal is designed to be flexible enough so that you can use it to build any type of database-backed website. Because of that flexibility, and because Drupal is written in PHP, there are many things that are possible to do in Drupal programming, but which amount to a misuse of the Drupal API and are therefore definitely not recommended. Many API misuse mistakes are covered in this book:

- Hacking code instead of using hooks: "Principle: Drupal Is Alterable" (page 9)
- "Mistake: Executing Code on Every Page Load" (page 42) (just below)
- "Mistake: Using an Overly General Hook" (page 43) (later in this section)
- Using t() to internationalize user-entered text: "Internationalizing User-Entered Text" (page 18)
- Using db_query() for complex queries: "Querying the Database with the Database API" (page 24)
- Over-cleansing user-provided input: "Cleansing and Checking User-Provided Input" (page 28)

Mistake: Executing Code on Every Page Load

One of the most drastic misuses of the Drupal API that new Drupal programmers can make is to write PHP code and place it either in the main body of a module (outside all function definitions, so that it gets executed every time the module is loaded), or in an implementation of hook_boot() or hook_init() (both of which run early in the page generation process on most or all page loads). While this practice might be a good idea in a custom PHP/MySQL site or in other CMS systems, Drupal generally has a different hook or method that can be used to accomplish the same purpose with less overhead (since it will be executed only when needed) and less programming (since you are taking advantage of Drupal's built-in logic, rather than recreating it). For example:

- Detecting an unauthorized user and redirecting to an error page: use the Drupal permissions system instead. You may also find the contributed "Redirect 403 to User Login" module useful.
- Detecting a particular URL and executing custom PHP code to generate output (HTML, AJAX, and so on): use the Drupal menu routing (URL registration) system instead.
- Overriding behavior that another module has defined for a particular URL: use hook_menu_alter() instead.
- Processing submitted form input: use the Drupal Form API instead.

Further reading and references:

- "Checking Drupal Permissions" (page 29)
- "Registering for URLs and Displaying Content" (page 50)
- hook_menu_alter(): "Altering a URL Registration" (page 53)
- "Generating Forms with the Form API" (page 59)
- Redirect 403 to User Login module: *http://drupal.org/project/r4032login*

Mistake: Using an Overly General Hook

Another API misuse mistake that many new Drupal programmers make is using an overly general hook when a more specific hook exists. This leads to your hook implementation function being executed more often than necessary. Your hook implementation function most likely will also be longer than necessary, because it will have more logic in it to detect the special case you are trying to handle.

The most common example of this is hook_form_alter(), which you can use to make alterations in forms provided by other modules. Use hook_form_FORM_ID_alter() instead:

```
// Bad - runs whenever any form is generated:
function mymodule_form_alter($form, $form_state, $form_id) {
  if ($form_id == 'othermodule_form') {
    // Alteration code here.
  }
}

// Good - runs when this specific form is generated:
function mymodule_form_othermodule_form_alter($form, $form_state) {
  // Alteration code here.
}
```

See "Generating Forms with the Form API" (page 59) for more on the Form API.

Mistake: Saving PHP Code in the Database

It is possible, by enabling certain modules and granting certain permissions, for users to include PHP code within the body of page or block content (and in other places), which is executed when the page or block is displayed. While this might seem like a great convenience and a time-saver, it is usually a mistake to allow this because of the following factors:

Security risk

PHP code can add, change, or delete files and database records (any PHP code run during a page request has full rights to change the database). So, granting this permission opens up the possibility of malicious PHP code being added to a block or a page.

Risk of bugs

Even if you only grant the permission to highly trusted users, they could, through a bug in their PHP code, alter files or database records by mistake (the code would only have to run once to cause problems).

Hard to debug

Even if the PHP code isn't dangerous, if it has a coding error, the page or block could sometimes produce the wrong output or cause a "White Screen of Death" (completely blank page), which is difficult to debug when it comes from PHP code stored in the database.

Hard to track

Allowing PHP code to be stored makes it hard to keep track of which page or block does what.

Luckily, there are good alternatives for the common reasons people might want to store PHP code in the database:

Control block visibility

Use the Context module or the Panels module, which allow you much more flexibility on block placement.

Database queries

Use the Views module.

Custom page or block output

Create your block or page in a module.

Change how something is displayed

Override a theme function.

Calculations for a field

Create your own custom field or formatter.

Related topics:

- "Avoiding Custom Programming with Fielded Data" (page 39)
- "Registering for URLs and Displaying Content" (page 50)
- "Programming with Hooks in Modules and Themes" (page 11)
- "Defining a Field Type" (page 75)

- "Programming with Field Formatters" (page 79)

Contributed modules mentioned in this section:

- Context: *http://drupal.org/project/context*
- Panels: *http://drupal.org/project/panels*
- Views: *http://drupal.org/project/views*

Mistake: Working Alone

One of the great strengths of the Drupal software is that it is produced by the Drupal open-source project, which is a world wide community of people who have chosen to come together and donate their time and money towards making Drupal better. The software has been around since 2001 or so, in which time the community of contributors has grown from one person (the founder and continuing leader of the Drupal project, Dries Buytaert) to thousands of people. And although it does have its disfunctional moments, the Drupal community often works together pretty well to create the core Drupal software and add-ons, write the documentation, and support Drupal users.

As a Drupal programmer, if you try to work alone without connecting to the Drupal community, you are making a mistake: engaging with the community will almost certainly directly help you become more effective and skillful in your Drupal endeavors. But if you engage with the Drupal community by thinking only about what you can get from the community, you are also making a mistake. Instead, engaging in a thoughtful and respectful way and thinking about how you can contribute to the Drupal community and project as well as your own needs will get you better results (people are more likely to help someone who has this type of attitude). Furthermore, if you are able to engage in ways that contribute to the Drupal project and community, you will reap the benefits, in the future, of improving your own skills, and also having better software to use.

Participating in Groups

One of the best ways to connect to the Drupal community is to join a local Drupal user group and participate in meetings and events that members of the group organize. At these events, you may learn techniques that you can apply to your own work, or you may be inspired by seeing what others have done with Drupal; many local Drupal groups also encourage members to ask each other questions using forums or online IRC chats. If you live in or near a city without a local group, or if the local group does not have meetings, you could also consider organizing a meeting, which could be as simple as choosing a coffee shop and setting a time for people to gather to talk about Drupal or show off the projects they are working on. There are also world wide groups organized around topics and languages, which come together primarily on forums and on IRC.

Next steps:

- Find a regional or topical group to join: *http://groups.drupal.org*
- Learn about IRC: *http://drupal.org/irc*

Reporting Issues and Contributing Code to the Drupal Community

Another key way to connect to the Drupal community is to use the Drupal *issue queues* (known as bug databases or ticket systems in other projects) to report software bugs and request new features. Each project (Drupal core, contributed modules, contributed themes, and contributed Drupal distributions) has its own issue queue, so the first step in reporting an issue is to narrow down exactly what project the issue pertains to. Then, visit that project's home page on drupal.org, and search to make sure the issue has not already been reported; if it has, you can subscribe to the existing issue, perhaps adding a comment if you are seeing the same problem from a slightly different cause or in a slightly different environment than previously reported. Finally, if what you would like to report is a new issue, click the "Create a new issue" link on the project's issue search results page, and fill in the issue details.

Subscribing to Issues

The drupal.org website allows you to subscribe to individual issues or to entire projects' issues. To subscribe to an individual issue, click on the "Follow" button on the issue page, and you should receive an email message whenever someone adds a new comment to the issue. To subscribe to the issues for an entire project, or to check your issue notification settings, visit your user account page on drupal.org, and click on Notifications (at a minimum, make sure it is set up to send you email notifications for issues that you follow).

To ensure that your issue reports are well-received, consider these points:

Be polite and respectful
>   Drupal is open-source, community-produced software, so for the most part it is created by volunteers. Sounding angry or disgusted in your issue report is not likely to inspire the volunteer who created the software that has the bug to fix it.

Be constructive
>   If possible, suggest a solution rather than just pointing out the problem.

Be clear and complete

If you report a vague problem like "This doesn't work," without details of what you were doing, what you observed happening, and why you think what you observed was not correct, your report is likely to be ignored or marked "cannot reproduce."

Be attentive

Often, the maintainer of the component or project you are reporting the issue on will have questions for you, such as whether you have certain other modules installed on your site. They will ask the questions as comment replies to your original issue; your quick response to any questions will expedite action to resolve the issue.

Issues are also the starting point for contributing code to the Drupal project, since most (ideally, all) code changes in Drupal core and add-on projects are coordinated on issues. To contribute suggested code changes, first file an issue report, and then create and attach a *patch* file to the issue. After attaching a patch, be attentive—it's highly unlikely that your patch will be accepted without some changes, and it's much more likely that your patch will eventually be accepted if you follow the issue and make the requested changes, rather than just dropping the patch on the issue and hoping that someone else will finalize it. Keep in mind these additional points:

- It is in your interest to get the code *committed* (added to the project): presumably you want the new feature or want to have the bug fixed. So, do everything you can to get it committed (make changes suggested by reviewers).

- Patches that don't follow the Drupal coding standards, that have security problems, or that don't follow standard Drupal programming practices are unlikely to be committed.

- The priorities of the project maintainer or patch reviewer may be different from yours, but they do have final say. For instance, they may decide that they don't want to add complexity to their module, if you propose a new feature, or they may suggest that you submit your patch (or idea) to a different project. So, be prepared to be flexible.

Further reading and references:

- Novice contributor guide to patches: *http://drupal.org/novice*
- Git revision control system: *http://drupal.org/documentation/git*
- Drupal project coding standards: *http://drupal.org/coding-standards*

Contributing to the Drupal Community in Other Ways

Programmers naturally think about contributing code to the project, but there are many other ways to contribute to the project and to the community, which are all valuable. Some ideas:

- Write or edit Drupal documentation: see *http://drupal.org/contribute/documenta tion*
- Attend a DrupalCon or regional conference and make a presentation to share your Drupal knowledge: see *http://groups.drupal.org/calendar*
- If you speak a non-English language, translate Drupal software into your language: see *http://localize.drupal.org*
- Join or donate to the Drupal Association, the non-profit organization that keeps the drupal.org servers running, organizes DrupalCon events, and generally works for the benefit of the Drupal project: see *http://association.drupal.org*

CHAPTER 4

Drupal Programming Examples

Now that you have learned the basic principles of Drupal programming and how to avoid making common Drupal programming mistakes, it's time to put your programming skills to work! This section of the book covers special topics in Drupal programming that you can use to enhance websites built with Drupal. My advice would be to skim the sections of this chapter now so you know what is there, and then read them in more detail when you need them.

I chose these particular examples because they are all things I've actually needed to do in my freelance work as a Drupal site builder and my volunteer work programming for the Drupal project. Actually, they cover nearly all of the programming I've needed to do as a freelance site builder, given that I tend to use existing contributed modules wherever I can, rather than jumping straight into programming at every opportunity. And in the realm of volunteer work that I've done for the Drupal project, which has included writing and maintaining contributed modules on drupal.org, custom programming for the drupal.org website, and providing patches for Drupal core and contributed modules, the "Registering for URLs and Displaying Content" (page 50) section covers the common threads.

Further programming examples:

- The Drupal core code itself, which includes extensive documentation and tests
- The Examples for Developers project, *http://drupal.org/project/examples*, which has comprehensive coverage of the Drupal core APIs and how to use them in your own modules
- Thousands of GPL-licensed contributed modules you can download from *http://drupal.org/project/modules* and then adapt for your own work

- The API reference site, *http://api.drupal.org*, and this book's guide on how to make the best use of it: "Using api.drupal.org" (page 97)

Registering for URLs and Displaying Content

"How Drupal Handles URL Requests" (page 4) contains an overview of how Drupal 7 handles URL requests and returns content to a web browser or other requester. This section of the book goes into more detail about how a module you write can be part of that process, by registering with Drupal to handle specific URLs, by providing page and block content, and by generating and processing HTML forms.

 Given that Drupal has many hooks and that it is written in PHP, there are many ways that you could consider writing code for Drupal that would return output in response to a URL request, or that would place content in a region on a page or set of pages. Most of these ways would, however, amount to subverting Drupal's standard processes, rather than working within the Drupal framework. Use the methods in this section of the book for best results.

In Drupal 7 and earlier versions of Drupal, assuming that you have decided you need your module to output some content, the first choice you need to make is whether to provide a *menu router* entry or a *block*. A menu router entry allows you to respond to a URL request by providing the main HTML content for that page, or in some cases, the entire output for the URL (such as XML output that is used by a Flash script on your site, an RSS feed, or an AJAX response). A block allows you to provide a chunk of output that can be placed on one or more of a site's HTML-based pages. In either case, you will need to register with Drupal for the block or URL, and then write a function to generate the output; in the case of a menu router entry, you will also need to define permissions for accessing the URL. All of these steps are described in the following sections.

Note that you should only write code to provide blocks and menu router entries if there is some logic or programming needed to generate the content of the block or page. If you are displaying static content, you can create a block or content item using Drupal's user interface, and if you need to employ some logic to decide where or when to show the block, use the Context module or Panels module. Also, keep in mind that using the Views module is a better choice than making a custom module in many cases.

Further reading:

- "Mistake: Programming Too Much" (page 35)
- "Avoiding Custom Programming with Fielded Data" (page 39)

Drupal 8

The menu router system and block placement systems will be quite different in Drupal 8. As of this writing, the system that is envisioned is expected to have the following elements:

- When defining a block in Drupal 8, you will be able to define additional context information that is needed in order to decide what content to display.

- Drupal 7 uses the concept of a special "main page content" block (which modules register to provide at different URLs). In Drupal 8, all page elements will be blocks on equal footing, with no particular "main" block.

- In Drupal 8, URL registration will correspond to *layouts*, which determine which blocks are displayed where under which context conditions.

Registering for a URL

To register to provide the main page content for a URL, define a menu router entry by implementing hook_menu() in your *mymodule.module* file First, you will need to choose a URL, with the following considerations:

- If you are providing an administrative page, the URL should be chosen to place the page in an appropriate, existing section of the Drupal core administration screens. For instance, if it's "structural," it should start with admin/structure/, and if it's for use by developers, it should start with admin/config/development/. You can see a complete list of the sections in function system_menu() in the *modules/system/system.module* file that comes with Drupal.

- Make sure your URL does not conflict with a URL that another module might provide. Normally, prefixing with or including your module's short name is a good idea (mymodule in this example).

- Make your URL like others in Drupal. For instance, if you are defining an autocomplete responder for a form, make the URL mymodule/autocomplete, similar to the existing user/autocomplete URL defined by the core User module.

- The URL can contain *wildcards*. For example, the core Node module defines a URL of node/ followed by the node content item's ID number.

After choosing your URL, implement hook_menu() to tell Drupal about it:

```
function mymodule_menu() {
  $items = array();
```

```
  // Put the chosen URL here, minus the base site URL.
  $items['mymodule/mypath'] = array(
    'title' => 'My page title',
    // Function that will generate the content.
    'page callback' => 'mymodule_page_generate',
    // Function used to check permissions. This defaults to user_access(),
    // which is provided here as an illustration -- you can omit this line
    // if you want to use the user_access() function. Put the name of your
    // custom access check function here if you have one.
    'access callback' => 'user_access',
    // Arguments needed for your access callback function. If using the
    // default user_access() function, the argument is the name of the
    // permission a user must have to access the page.
    'access arguments' => array('access content'),
  );

  return $items;
}
```

Notes:

- The hook_menu() implementation references a page-generating function
  (mymodule_page_generate() in this example). Since block-generating functions
  are very similar to page-generating functions, the details of what this function
  should return are covered in a separate section below: "Providing Page and Block
  Output" (page 55).

- There is no need to explicitly check for access permissions in your page-generating
  function or elsewhere, assuming that you set up an *access callback* in your
  hook_menu() implementation. Drupal will verify and run this access check for you
  automatically and return a 403 access denied response for unauthorized users.

Auto-Loading, Arguments, and Wildcards in hook_menu()

The menu routing system in Drupal is fairly powerful, and one of the powerful features
that new Drupal programmers often don't know about is the ability to auto-load objects.
Using this feature takes several steps:

1. Use a wildcard in the URL you are registering for, and give it a name. Wildcards in
   hook_menu() URLs start with %, so for instance you could register for a URL like
   'mymodule/%mymodule_object'.

2. Define a function of the same name as your wildcard with a load suffix:
   mymodule_object_load() in this example. It should load your object and return it.

---

3. When someone goes to a specific URL matching your pattern, such as *example.com/mymodule/123*, your load function will be called with the corresponding piece of the URL as its first argument ('123' in this example). You can tell Drupal to pass additional arguments to this function by adding a 'load arguments' element to your hook_menu() implementation.

4. In 'page arguments', 'access arguments', and related elements of your hook_menu() implementation, you can pass the loaded object by using the numeric index of your wildcard in the URL. In URL 'mymodule/%mymodule_object', for example, the 0 placeholder would have value 'mymodule' and the 1 placeholder would have your loaded object. So if your page-generating function has two arguments, the object and a view mode, you might put 'page callback' => array(1, 'full'), into your hook_menu() implementation to indicate this.

There is an example that uses an auto-loading wildcard in Step 4 of "Defining an Entity Type" (page 68).

Further reading and references:

- "Programming with Hooks in Modules and Themes" (page 11)
- "Drupal core's main permission system" (page 29)
- The Page example in Examples for Developers: *http://drupal.org/project/examples*
- Look up hook_menu() on *http://api.drupal.org* for complete documentation of all its options.

Altering a URL Registration

A related task that you may need to do in a module is to alter how another module has registered for a URL. One common reason would be that you want to use a different access permission system for the URL. To do this, implement hook_menu_alter() in your *mymodule.module* file. For example:

```
function mymodule_menu_alter(&$items) {
  // $items contains all items from hook_menu() implementations.
  $items['other/module/path']['access callback'] = 'mymodule_check_access';
}

function mymodule_check_access() {
  // The user who is trying to access the page.
  global $user;

  // Calculate whether this user should get access or not,
  // and return TRUE or FALSE.
}
```

Further reading and references:

- Look up hook_menu() on *http://api.drupal.org* for complete documentation of all its options (which can be used in hook_menu_alter() too).
- "Programming with Hooks in Modules and Themes" (page 11)
- "Drupal core's main permission system" (page 29)

Registering a Block

If you want to provide content that can be displayed on multiple pages, you should register for a block rather than for a URL in your module. To register for a block, you need to implement hook_block_info() in your *mymodule.module* file to tell Drupal about the existence of your block, and then implement hook_block_view() to generate the block content. For example:

```
// Tell Drupal about your block.
function mymodule_block_info() {
  $blocks = array();

  // The array key is known as the block "delta" (a unique identifier
  // within your module), and is used in other block hooks. Choose
  // something descriptive.
  $blocks['first_block'] = array(
    // The name shown on the Blocks administration page.
    // Be descriptive and unique across all blocks.
    'info' => t('First block from My Module'),
  );

  return $blocks;
}

// Generate the block content. Note that the $delta value passed in
// is the same as the array key you returned in your hook_block_info()
// implementation.
function mymodule_block_view($delta = '') {
  if ($delta == 'first_block') {
    return array(
      // The block's title.
      'subject' => t('First block'),
      // The block's content.
      'content' => mymodule_block_generate(),
    );
  }
}
```

Notes:

- Implementations of hook_block_info() can be more complex than this: they can specify cache parameters (block output is cached by default for efficiency) and default placement.
- Blocks can also have configuration settings.
- The hook_block_view() implementation here calls a function (in this example, mymodule_block_generate()) to provide the actual block content. Since block-generating functions are very similar to page-generating functions, the details of what this function should return are covered in a separate section below: "Providing Page and Block Output" (page 55).
- After adding a new block to a hook_block_info() implementation, you will need to clear the Drupal cache to make it visible.

Further reading, examples, and references:

- "Programming with Hooks in Modules and Themes" (page 11)
- "The Drupal Cache" (page 6)
- The Block example in Examples for Developers (*http://drupal.org/project/exam ples*) and many Drupal core blocks include configuration options, cache settings, and other options.
- Look up hook_block_info() on *http://api.drupal.org* to find all the options and links to the Drupal core functions that implement it.

Providing Page and Block Output

Once your module has registered for a page or block (see previous sections), you need to write a function that returns the page or block output. In Drupal 6 and prior versions, this type of function would return a fully rendered text string containing both the data to display and the HTML markup. In Drupal 7, there has been a change in philosophy, however, and it is currently recommended that page and block functions return a *render array*, which contains the data to output along with formatting information.

Here is the general structure of a render array that you could return from a page- or block-generating function:

```
$output = array(
  'sensible_identifier_1' => array(
    '#type' => 'element_identifier',
    // Other properties and data here.
  ),
  'sensible_identifier_2' => array(
    '#theme' => 'theme_hook',
```

```
      // Other properties and data here.
    ),
    // Other pieces of output here.
  );
```

Notes:

- The outermost array keys are arbitrary: choose sensible identifiers that will remind you of what each piece of your block or page is.

- At the next level of arrays, keys starting with '#' are *property* keys that are recognized by the Render API.

- Each sub-array needs to either have a '#type' property, whose value is the machine name of a *render element*, or a '#theme' property, whose value is the name of a theme hook.

- Render elements are basically sets of properties in an array that correspond to one or more HTML elements. They are defined in modules by implementing hook_element_info(); many of them are form elements. Each render element requires one or more other properties to be provided and may have optional properties that you can use to control the output.

- Theme hooks are defined by modules by implementing hook_theme(), and each theme hook also requires one or more properties to be provided.

- Be sure that all your text is internationalized.

Here's an example of a render array that has an informational paragraph, followed by a list of items, followed by a table (the paragraph uses a 'markup' render element; the list and table use the 'item_list' and 'table' theme hooks):

```
$output = array(
  'introduction' => array(
    '#type' => 'markup',
    '#markup' => '<p>' . t('General information goes here.') . '</p>',
  ),
  'colors' => array(
    '#theme' => 'item_list',
    '#items' => array(t('Red'), t('Blue'), t('Green')),
    '#title' => t('Colors'),
  ),
  'materials' => array(
    '#theme' => 'table',
    '#caption' => t('Materials'),
    '#header' => array(t('Material'), t('Characteristic')),
    '#rows' => array(
      array(t('Steel'), t('Strong')),
```

```
              array(t('Aluminum'), t('Light')),
          ),
       ),
    );
```

Further reading and references:

- More about forms: "Generating Forms with the Form API" (page 59)
- More about theme hooks: "Making Your Output Themeable" (page 13)
- Internationalizing text: "Principle: Drupal Is International" (page 16)
- Unfortunately, there is not currently a comprehensive reference for Drupal render elements (although one is in planning as of this writing). Modules register to provide render elements by implementing `hook_element_info()`. For example, `system_element_info()` provides most of the Drupal core elements, such as `'link'` and `'markup'`, which are used in many render arrays. Look up `hook_ele ment_info()` on *http://api.drupal.org* to find Drupal core functions that provide render elements, and click through to find out what elements each module provides.
- Find Drupal core theme hooks on the "Default theme implementations" topic page on *http://api.drupal.org*.

 It is still possible in Drupal 7 to return strings from your page and block content functions instead of render arrays. Using render arrays is preferred, however, because:

- They are self-documenting.
- They allow modules to use `hook_page_alter()` to alter the page before it is rendered.
- They leave final rendering until late in the page generation process, so unnecessary rendering can be avoided if a particular section of the page is not actually displayed.

Generating paged output

If a page or block you are generating output for is listing data, you need to think about what should happen if the list of data gets long; usually you would want the output to be separated into pages. If you are using a database query to generate the list, Drupal's Database API and theme system make separating the output into pages very easy. Here are the steps:

1. Use a dynamic query with `db_select()`, rather than a static query with `db_query()`.
2. Add the `PagerDefault` *extension* to your database query.

3. Add theme('pager') to your output, either directly or as part of a render array. This will add links to the pages of output, which will make use of a URL query parameter called 'page' on the base URL of the page. The PagerDefault extension will read this URL query parameter to figure out what page the user is on, and return the appropriate rows in the database query automatically.

As an example, assume you want to show the titles of the most recently updated node content items, and you want to show 10 items per page. Here is the code you would need to put into your output-generating function for the block or page:

```
// Find the most recently updated nodes.
$query = db_select('node', 'n')
  ->fields('n', array('title'))
  ->orderBy('n.changed', 'DESC')
  // Be sure to check permissions, and only show published items.
  ->addTag('node_access')
  ->condition('n.status', 1)
  // Put this last, because the return value is a new object.
  ->extend('PagerDefault');
// This only applies with the PagerDefault extension.
$query->limit(10);
$result = $query->execute();

// Extract and sanitize the information from the query result.
$titles = array();
foreach ($result as $row) {
  $titles[] = check_plain($row->title);
}

// Make the render array for a paged list of titles.
$build = array();
// The list of titles.
$build['items'] = array(
  '#theme' => 'item_list',
  '#items' => $titles,
);
// The pager.
$build['item_pager'] = array('#theme' => 'pager');

return $build;
```

Further reading and references:

- "Dynamic queries" (page 25)
- "Cleansing and Checking User-Provided Input" (page 28)
- It is usually better to use the Views module rather than doing your own page queries: "Avoiding Custom Programming with Fielded Data" (page 39)

Generating Forms with the Form API

One of the real strengths of Drupal for programmers is the Form API, which has been in place with very little change through several versions of Drupal (it is not expected to change in Drupal 8 either). The basic idea of the Form API is that instead of writing the HTML for a form directly, you create a form-generating function that returns a structured form array. Form arrays have the same structure as the render arrays discussed in the previous section, and they contain information about the form elements along with their attributes (labels, sizes, etc.). Then you write separate functions that tell Drupal how to validate and process form submissions. The advantages of using the Form API over doing all of this in raw HTML and PHP are:

- You have to write a lot less code, since you're letting Drupal handle all of the standard parts of form creation and submission.

- Your code will be easier to read and maintain.

- As with other parts of Drupal, your form will be alterable by other modules and the exact rendering is controlled by the theme system.

- When the form is rendered, Drupal adds a unique token to protect against cross-site scripting, and this is validated during form submission.

Here is a simple example of a form-generating function:

```
function mymodule_personal_data_form(&$form, &$form_state) {
  $form = array();

  // Plain text input element for first name.
  $form['first_name'] = array(
    '#type' => 'textfield',
    '#title' => t('First name'),
  );

  // Plain text element for company name, only visible to some
  // users.
  $form['company'] = array(
    '#type' => 'textfield',
    '#title' => t('Company'),
    // This assumes permission 'use company field' has been defined.
    '#access' => user_access('use company field'),
  );

  // Some hidden information to be used later.
  $form['information'] = array(
    '#type' => 'value',
    '#value' => $my_information,
  );

  // Submit button.
  $form['submit'] = array(
```

```
      '#type' => 'submit',
      '#value' => t('Submit'),
    );

    return $form;
  }
```

Notes:

- The notes about render arrays from "Providing Page and Block Output" (page 55) also apply to form arrays.

- The 'value' form element type can be used to pass information to the form validation and submission functions. This information is not rendered at all into the form's HTML, in contrast to 'hidden' form elements (which render as HTML 'input' elements with type attribute 'hidden'), so they are more secure and can contain any PHP data structure.

- Form elements have an '#access' property; if its value is FALSE, the form element is not presented to this user. If omitted, it defaults to TRUE.

- The function arguments are $form (the form array) and $form_state (an array of state information), followed by any additional input arguments that your form needs. The state information is carried through the form validation and submission process.

Creating a form array is just one step in the process of displaying and processing form input. To set up a form in your module, you will need to do the following:

1. Choose an ID name for your form, which should typically start with your module name. For example, you might choose mymodule_personal_data_form.

2. Create a form generating function with the same name, which returns the form array (see previous example).

3. If necessary, to validate form submissions, create a form validation function mymodule_personal_data_form_validate(). This function should call form_set_error() if the submission is invalid, and it should do nothing if all is well.

4. Create a form submission function mymodule_personal_data_form_submit() to process the form submissions (save information to the database and so on). For example:

```
function mymodule_personal_data_form_submit(&$form, &$form_state) {
  // The values submitted by the user are in $form_state['values'].
  // They need to be sanitized.
  $name = check_plain($form_state['values']['first_name']);
  // Values you stored in the form array are also available.
```

```
    $info = $form_state['values']['information'];

    // Your processing code goes here, such as saving this to the database.
}
```

5. Call `drupal_get_form('mymodule_personal_data_form')` to build the form—do not call your form-generating function directly. Your validation and submission functions will be called automatically when a user submits the form. If your form is the sole content of a page whose URL you are registering for in a `hook_menu()` implementation, you can use `drupal_get_form()` as the page-generating function:

```
// Inside your hook_menu() implementation:
$item['mymodule/my_form_page'] = array(
  'page callback' => 'drupal_get_form',
  'page arguments' => array('mymodule_personal_data_form'),
  // Don't forget the access information, title, etc.!
);
```

Further reading, examples, and resources:

- The Form example from the Examples for Developers project: *http://drupal.org/project/examples*
- Form-generating functions in Drupal core are listed in the "Form builder functions" topic on *http://api.drupal.org*
- `hook_menu()`: "Registering for a URL" (page 51)
- "Drupal core's main permission system" (page 29)

 Be careful about caching form output, because `drupal_get_form()` adds verification information to the form output, and this information is invalid after some time has passed. If your form is displayed in a block, be sure that the block is not cached; this is not a problem if the form is part of the main page content.

Using confirmation forms

For security reasons, it is important to verify destructive actions connected with a URL. For instance, if your module has a URL that allows an administrative user to delete some data or a file, you should confirm this intention before deleting the data. The reason is that the user could have been tricked into visiting that URL by a hacking attack.

Drupal makes this type of confirmation easy. Here are the steps:

1. Instead of registering your URL with a function that performs the deletion directly, use `drupal_get_form()` as the page callback, passing in the name of a form-generating function.

2. Have your form-generating function call `confirm_form()` to generate a confirmation form.

3. Perform the data deletion in the form submission function, which will only be called if the action is confirmed.

Here's an example of the code:

```
// The menu router registration.
function mymodule_menu() {
  // ...

  // Assume there is a content ID number.
  $items['admin/content/mycontent/delete/%'] = array(
    'title' => 'Delete content item?',
    'page callback' => 'drupal_get_form',
    // Pass the content ID number to the form generating function.
    'page arguments' => array('mymodule_confirm_delete', 4),
    'access arguments' => array('delete mycontent items'),
  );

  // ...
}

// Form-generating function.
function mymodule_confirm_delete($form, $form_state, $id) {
  // Save the ID for the submission function.
  $form['mycontent_id'] = array(
    '#type' => 'value',
    '#value' => $id,
  );

  return confirm_form($form,
    // You could load the item and display the title here.
    t('Are you sure you want to delete content item %id?',
      array('%id' => $id)),
    // The URL path to return to if the user cancels.
    'admin/content/mycontent');
}

// Form-submission function.
function mymodule_confirm_delete_submit($form, $form_state) {
  // Read the ID saved in the form.
  $id = $form_state['values']['mycontent_id'];

  // Perform the data deletion.
  // ...
```

```
    // Redirect somewhere, for example the site home page.
    drupal_goto('<front>');
  }
```

Further reading and related topics:

- "Principle: Drupal Is Secure; User Input Is Insecure" (page 27)
- "Registering for a URL" (page 51)
- "Generating Forms with the Form API" (page 59)

Altering forms

One of the more common reasons for someone building a Drupal site to create a custom module is to alter a form that is displayed by Drupal core or another module. Typically, the reason is that the site owner or site designer decides they find some of the text on the form confusing, they want some part of the form hidden, they want to change the order of fields on a form, or they want some additional validation to be done on form submissions. All of these alterations can be done easily by using hook_form_alter() and related functions.

Before deciding you need a custom form-altering module, however, you should check to see if you can alter the form in a different way. Some core and contributed modules, for example, have configuration options that will let you alter labels on forms, and you can also use the String Overrides contributed module to make global text changes (such as changing all "Submit" buttons to say "Send"). If you want to add text at the top of a form, you might be able to use a block. Also, content editing forms are configurable in the administrative user interface: you can add help text to fields, change field labels, change the order of fields, add and remove fields from content types, and change the displayed name of the content type, among other settings. Each content type also has several settings for comments that affect the comment form, and there are many other examples of configuration options—so be sure to investigate before you start programming.

If you do need to alter a form via an alter hook in your custom module, here are the steps:

1. Figure out the form ID of the form you are altering. The easiest way to do this is to look at the HTML source of the page with the form—the ID will be the "id" attribute of the HTML form tag. For this example, let's assume the ID is 'the_form_id'.

2. Implement hook_form_FORM_ID_alter() by declaring a function called mymodule_form_the_form_id_alter() in your *module.module* file. Some forms, like field widget forms, use a different alter hook, such as hook_field_widget_form_alter(); these hooks work the same way as hook_form_FORM_ID_alter().

3. Alter the form array in this function.

As an example, assume that you want to change the user registration form on a site so that it only allows people to register using email addresses within your company's domain. The form ID in this case is 'user_register_form', and here is the alter function you would need to define:

```
// Form alteration.
function mymodule_form_user_register_form_alter(&$form, &$form_state, $form_id) {
  // Change the label on the email address field.
  $form['account']['mail']['#title'] = t('Company e-mail address');

  // Add a validation function.
  $form['#validate'][] = 'mymodule_validate_register_email';
}

// Validation function.
function mymodule_validate_register_email($form, $form_state) {
  $email = $form_state['values']['mail'];
  // Check that the email is within the company domain.
  // If not, call form_set_error('mail', t('message goes here'));
}
```

Further reading and related topics:

- "Programming with Field Widgets" (page 77)
- "Generating Forms with the Form API" (page 59)

Adding AJAX, JavaScript, and auto-complete to forms

A frequent need in web pages with forms is to have the form respond immediately to the user's actions via JavaScript or AJAX; a common special case of this is an auto-complete text field (where suggestions pop up as the user types in a text field). Drupal has specific mechanisms in its Form API to handle auto-completes and other AJAX and JavaScript use cases.

To make a text input field have auto-complete behavior, here are the steps:

1. Add an '#autocomplete_path' property to your 'textfield' form element array, with a URL path in it. This looks like:

```
// In a form-generating function:
$form['my_autocomplete_field'] = array(
  '#type' => 'textfield',
  '#autocomplete_path' => 'mymodule/autocomplete',
  '#title' => t('My field label'),
);
```

2. Register for this URL path in your hook_menu() implementation, referencing a page callback function name. This looks like:

```
// In your hook_menu() implementation:
$items['mymodule/autocomplete'] = array(
  'page callback' => 'mymodule_autocomplete',
  // Use an appropriate permission here.
  'access arguments' => array('access content'),
  'type' => MENU_CALLBACK,
);
```

3. Define the page callback function. It will take one argument (the string the user has typed), and should return an array of responses in JSON format, as in this example:

```
function mymodule_autocomplete($string = '') {
  $matches = array();
  if ($string) {
    // Sanitize $string and find appropriate matches -- about 10 or fewer.
    // Put them into $matches.
    // ...
  }

  drupal_json_output($matches);
}
```

Generic JavaScript code and files can be added to a form by using the '#attached' property. Drupal core includes the jQuery library, so you can make use of that when writing your JavaScript. Some examples:

```
// Attach a JavaScript file.
$form['#attached']['js'][] =
  drupal_get_path('module', 'mymodule') . '/mymodule.js';

// Attach some in-line JavaScript code.
$form['#attached']['js'][] = array(
  'type' => 'inline',
  'data' => $my_code,
);
```

Generic AJAX responses to a form element require adding a '#ajax' property to the form element, which defines a callback function to be called when the element changes, and the HTML ID of an area on the page to place the response. They are not covered in this book.

Further reading, examples, and resources:

- "Registering for a URL" (page 51)
- There are several examples of auto-completes in Drupal core, such as the author name field in node_form(), which auto-completes on user names at path 'user/ autocomplete'. This path is registered in user_menu() and its page callback function is user_autocomplete().
- There is also a complete standalone auto-complete example in the AJAX example in Examples for Developers (*http://drupal.org/project/examples*). File *ajax_example_autocomplete.inc* defines the forms and auto-complete callback functions, and function ajax_example_menu() in *ajax_example.module* registers the auto-complete paths.
- The AJAX example in the Examples for Developers project also shows how to do more generic AJAX responses.

Programming with Entities and Fields

This part of the book covers programming with Drupal entities and fields. The sections on defining entity types, field types, widgets, and formatters are independent of one another, so skim the terminology section first, and then you can skip to the section you need. The code samples in this part of the book complement, but do not duplicate, the well-documented Entity and Field examples from the Examples for Developers project.

Further reading and examples:

- "Avoiding Custom Programming with Fielded Data" (page 39)
- Entity example in Examples for Developers: *http://drupal.org/project/examples*
- Field example in Examples for Developers

 There is sometimes confusion between entity fields and database table fields. Within this section, the term "field" will always mean an entity field as defined in this section, and any references to database table fields will be clearly noted as such.

Terminology of Entities and Fields

As of Drupal version 7, Drupal core defines the concept of an *entity*, which stores data (such as content or settings) for a Drupal website. Drupal core version 7 defines four main user-visible *entity types*: *node* (for basic content), *taxonomy* (for classification of content), *comment* (for comments attached to content), and *user* (for user account information). Drupal 7 core also defines the *file* entity type, which is used internally to manage uploaded files. The Drupal API also allows modules to define additional entity types.

Each entity type can have one or more *bundles*, which are groupings of the *items* belonging to that entity type. For instance, the bundles of the node and comment entity types are *content types*, which an administrator can define within the Drupal user interface (modules can define them too); examples of content types are basic pages, news items, blog items, and forum posts. The bundles of the taxonomy entity type are *vocabularies*, and the items are the individual taxonomy terms; the user entity type has just one bundle, and its items are user accounts. Each entity item belongs to exactly one bundle.

Many entity types are *fieldable*, meaning that *fields* can be added to each bundle of the entity type (the fields can be different for each bundle within an entity type), and that each entity item will then have field values associated with it. Fields store additional information, which could be text, numbers, attached files, images, media URLs, or other data, and they can be single- or multiple-valued. Some entity types are not fieldable or do not allow administrators to change their fields; for example, an entity type used by a module for storing settings might define the fields and need to rely on those fields being present, so it would not want a user to be able to change them.

Each field has a *field type*, which defines what type of data the field stores; Drupal core defines several field types including one-line text, formatted long text, and images, and modules can define additional field types. When a field is *attached* to a bundle, it is known as a *field instance*, which encompasses the field type, an internal field identifier for programming use, a label, and other settings.

When a user is creating or editing an entity item, a field *widget* is used to receive the data on the entity editing form. For instance, a simple text field can use a normal HTML text input form field widget, or if its values are restricted to a small set, it could use an HTML select, radio buttons, or checkboxes. Drupal core defines the common widgets needed to edit its fields in standard ways, and modules can define their own widgets for their fields or other modules' fields. Widgets are assigned to each field instance when the field is attached to the bundle.

When an entity item is being displayed, a field *formatter* is used to display the data. For instance, a long text field could be formatted as plain text (with all HTML tags stripped out), passed through a text filter, or truncated to a particular length. Modules can define field formatters for their own or other modules' field types. Entity types can have *view modes* (such as *full page* and *teaser* for the node entity type), which allow entity items and their fields to be displayed differently under different circumstances. (Internal-use entity types do not need to have view modes, since these entity types' items are not directly displayed.) Formatters are assigned to each field instance for each view mode, or the field can be hidden in some or all view modes.

The data in entity items and their fields can be edited and translated, and many entity types keep track of *revisions*, making it possible to revert entity and field data to a prior version.

Defining an Entity Type

Before defining a new entity type, it is a good idea to think about whether you can instead use an existing entity type. For instance, if you need to store data that is basically site content, you should probably use the node entity type's API to define a new content type instead of defining your own entity type. This will be a lot less work, because the core Node module includes administrative screens and other functionality, and it will also allow you to use the many add-on modules that work with nodes.

One good use case for defining a new entity type is to store groups of settings for a module, which would allow the settings to be internationalized. Another good use case is to define storage for a set of content for a site that needs a completely different permissions system and display mechanism from the Drupal core node entity type, where the additional programming that would be needed to coerce the node entity type into doing what you want would be greater than the programming needed to define a separate entity type.

The remainder of this section shows how to define a new entity type. You might want to download the Entity example from the Examples for Developers project (*http:// drupal.org/project/examples*) and follow along there, or perhaps look at the code for one of the Drupal core entities.

Drupal 8

The code and process in this section is likely to be somewhat different in Drupal 8. In particular, it may not be necessary to use the contributed Entity API module, since some of its functionality may be included in Drupal core. Also, the page registration process will be different, so the code for that will need to change.

Step 1: Implement hook_entity_info()

The first step in defining a new entity type is to implement hook_entity_info() in your module. In Drupal 7, it is advisable to make use of the contributed Entity API module, since it takes care of many standard operations for you; you may also want to make use of the Entity Construction Kit module. To use the Entity API module, you'll need your module to have a dependency in its *mymodule.info* file:

```
dependencies[] = entity
```

With that taken care of, to define an entity type whose machine name is *myentity*, declare the following function in your *mymodule.module* file:

```
// Simple internal-use entity.
function mymodule_entity_info() {
  $return = array();

  $return['myentity'] = array(

    // Define basic information.
    'label' => t('Settings for My Module'),
    'plural label' => t('Settings for My Module'),
    'fieldable' => TRUE,

    // Provide information about the database table.
    'base table' => 'mymodule_myentity',
    'entity keys' => array(
      'id' => 'myentity_id',
      'label' => 'title',
    ),

    // Use classes from the Entity API module.
    'entity class' => 'Entity',
    'controller class' => 'EntityAPIController',

    // Have Entity API set up an administrative UI.
    'admin ui' => array(
        'path' => 'admin/myentity',
    ),
    'module' => 'mymodule',
    'access callback' => 'mymodule_myentity_access',

    // For content-type entities only.
    'uri callback' => 'mymodule_myentity_uri',
  );

  return $return;
}

// For content-type entities, return the URI for an entity.
function mymodule_myentity_uri($entity) {
```

```
    return array(
      'path' => 'myentity/' . $entity->myentity_id,
    );
  }
```

Step 2: Implement hook_schema()

The next step, for both simple and more complex entity types, is to implement
hook_schema() in your *mymodule.install* file, to set up the database table for storing
your entity information. The table name and some of the database field names need to
match what you put into your hook_entity_info() implementation, and you'll also
want a database field for language (assuming that you want your entity items to be
translatable), and possibly additional database fields to keep track of when entity items
are created and last updated. Here's the schema for the internal-use entity type example:

```
function mymodule_schema() {
  $schema = array();

  $schema['mymodule_myentity'] = array(
    'description' => 'Storage for myentity entity: settings for mymodule',
    'fields' => array(
      'myentity_id' => array(
        'description' => 'Primary key: settings ID.',
        'type' => 'serial',
        'unsigned' => TRUE,
        'not null' => TRUE,
      ),
      'title' => array(
        'description' => 'Label assigned to this set of settings',
        'type' => 'varchar',
        'length' => 200,
        'default' => '',
      ),
      'language' => array(
        'description' => 'Language of this set of settings',
        'type' => 'varchar',
        'length' => 12,
        'not null' => TRUE,
        'default' => '',
      ),
      // Consider adding additional fields for time created, time updated.
    ),
    'primary key' => array('myentity_id'),
    'indexes' => array(
      'language' => array('language'),
      // Add indexes for created/updated here too.
    ),
  );

  return $schema;
}
```

Step 3: Add pre-defined fields in hook_install()

If you are defining an entity type to use for settings, the next step is to attach fields to your entity bundle to store the settings you need. For a content-type entity, you may want to just let administrators add the fields in the administrative user interface (the Entity API module provides the URLs and screens), in which case you can skip this step. To add fields programmatically, implement hook_install() in your *mymodule.install* file, using Drupal core Field API functions:

```
function mymodule_install() {
  // Create a plain text field for a setting.
  $field = field_create_field(array(
    'field_name' => 'myentity_setting_1',
    'type' => 'text',
    'entity_types' => array('myentity'),
    'locked' => TRUE,
    'translatable' => TRUE,
  ));

  // Attach the field to the entity bundle.
  $instance = field_create_instance(array(
    'field_name' => 'myentity_setting_1',
    'entity_type' => 'myentity',
    'bundle' => 'myentity',
    'label' => t('Setting 1'),
    'description' => t('Help for this setting'),
    'required' => TRUE,
    'widget' => array(
      'type' => 'text_textfield',
    ),
    'display' => array(
      'default' => array(
        'label' => 'above',
        'type' => 'text_default',
      ),
    ),
  ));

  // Repeat these two function calls for each additional field.
}
```

Step 4: Set up display

The next step is to set up your entity type so that its items can be displayed, which is only necessary for a content-type entity. Given the URL callback function mymodule_myentity_uri() that was declared in Step 1, what we need to do is to register for the URL it returns, and tell Drupal to use the Entity API module's entity_view() function to display the entity:

```
function mymodule_menu() {
  $items = array();
```

```
// Register for the URL that mymodule_myentity_uri() returns.
// The wildcard %entity_object in the URL is handled by the Entity
// API function entity_object_load().
$items['myentity/%entity_object'] = array(
  // entity_object_load() needs to know what the entity type is.
  'load arguments' => array('myentity'),
  // This callback function, defined below, gives the page title.
  'title callback' => 'mymodule_myentity_page_title',
  // Use the Entity API function entity_view() to display the page.
  'page callback' => 'entity_view',
  // Pass in the loaded entity object from the URL.
  'page arguments' => array(1),
  // This access callback function is defined in Step 5.
  // Its arguments are the operation being attempted and
  // the loaded object.
  'access callback' => 'mymodule_myentity_access',
  'access arguments' => array('view', array(1)),
);

  return $items;
}

// Title callback function registered above.
function mymodule_myentity_page_title($entity) {
  return $entity->title;
}
```

Step 5: Set up editing and management

Both internal-use and content entity types need management pages and forms for creating and editing entity items. The Entity API module sets these up for you using the
information that you provided in your hook_entity_info() implementation (in step
1). There are several functions that you do need to define though:

- An access callback (which defines access permissions for your entity type). The
  function name is provided in your hook_entity_info() and hook_menu() implementations. You'll also need to implement hook_permission() to define
  permissions.
- A function to generate the entity item editing form, which must be called
  myentity_form(). A corresponding form submission handler is also needed. Your
  form needs to handle editing the title and the language, and then it needs to call
  field_attach_form() to let the Field module add the other fields to the form.

Here is the code for these functions:

```
// Define the permissions.
function mymodule_permission() {
  return array(
```

```php
      'view myentity' => array(
        'title' => t('View my entity content'),
      ),
      'administer myentity' => array(
        'title' => t('Administer my entities'),
      ),
   );
}

// Access callback for Entity API.
function mymodule_myentity_access($op, $entity, $account = NULL) {
  // $op is 'view', 'update', 'create', etc.
  // $entity could be NULL (to check access for all entity items)
  // or it could be a single entity item object.
  // $account is either NULL or a user object.

  // In this simple example, just check permissions for
  // viewing or administering the entity type generically.
  if ($op == 'view') {
    return user_access('view myentity', $account);
  }
  return user_access('administer myentity', $account);
}

// Form-generating function for the editing form.
function myentity_form($form, $form_state, $entity) {
  $form['title'] = array(
    '#title' => t('Title'),
    '#type' => 'textfield',
    '#default_value' => isset($entity->title) ? $entity->title : '',
  );

  // Build language options list.
  $default = language_default();
  $options = array($default->language => $default->name);
  if (module_exists('locale')) {
    $options = array(LANGUAGE_NONE => t('All languages')) +
      locale_language_list('name');
  }

  // Add language selector or value to the form.
  $langcode = isset($entity->language) ? $entity->language : '';
  if (count($options) > 1) {
    $form['language'] = array(
      '#type' => 'select',
      '#title' => t('Language'),
      '#options' => $options,
      '#default_value' => $langcode,
    );
  }
  else {
    $form['language'] = array(
```

```
      '#type' => 'value',
      '#value' => $langcode,
    );
  }

  $form['actions'] = array('#type' => 'actions');
  $form['actions']['submit'] = array(
    '#type' => 'submit',
    '#value' => t('Save'),
    '#weight' => 999,
  );

  field_attach_form('myentity', $entity, $form, $form_state, $langcode);

  return $form;
}

// Form submission handler for editing form.
function myentity_form_submit($form, &$form_state) {
  // Make use of Entity API class.
  $entity = entity_ui_form_submit_build_entity($form, $form_state);
  $entity->save();

  // Redirect to the management page.
  $form_state['redirect'] = 'admin/myentity';
}
```

Further reading, reference, related topics, and examples:

- "Programming with Hooks in Modules and Themes" (page 11)
- "Internationalizing User-Entered Text" (page 18)
- "Setting Up Database Tables: Schema API and hook_update_N()" (page 22)
- "Registering for a URL" (page 51)
- "Auto-Loading, Arguments, and Wildcards in hook_menu()" (page 52)
- "Checking Drupal Permissions" (page 29)
- "Generating Forms with the Form API" (page 59)
- Entity example in Examples for Developers: *http://drupal.org/project/examples*. Note that this example is a bit different from what is illustrated here, because it does not make use of the contributed Entity API module.
- The Node example in Examples for Developers shows how to create a content type for the core Node entity in a module.
- Entity API module: *http://drupal.org/project/entity*
- Entity Construction Kit module: *http://drupal.org/project/eck*

Defining a Field Type

If you need to attach data to nodes or other entity types, you need to find a field type that stores this type of data. Between Drupal core and contributed modules, there are field types available for most of the common use cases for fielded content (plain text, numbers, formatted text, images, media attachments, etc.), so if you need to store a particular type of data, start by searching contributed modules for a field type that will suit your needs. Keep in mind that the field type only defines the stored *data*, while the formatter defines the display of the data and the widget defines the method for data input. So instead of defining a field, you may only need a custom widget or formatter for your use case. Here are several examples:

- You need to store plain text data, based on clicking in a region on an image or using a Flash-based custom input method. For this use case, use a core Text field for storage, and create a custom widget for data input.

- You need to select one of several predefined choices on input, and display a predefined icon or canned text on output based on that choice. For this use case, use a core Number field for storage, and a core Select widget for input (with text labels; you could also use a core Text field for storage). Create a custom formatter for display.

- You are creating a website that displays company profiles, using a "Company" node content type. For each company content item, you need to attach several office locations. For this use case, use the contributed Geofield, Location, Address Field, or another geographical information field module rather than defining your own custom field (search module category Location to find more).

- For this same Company content type, you need several related fields to be grouped together on input and display; for instance, you might want to group the company size, annual revenue, and other similar fields together under "Statistics." For this use case, use the Field Group contributed module to group the fields rather than creating a custom field type module.

- For this same Company content type, you need to keep track of staff people, where each staff person has a profile with several fields. For this use case, create a separate Staff node content type, and use the contributed Entity Reference or Relation module to relate staff people to companies or companies to staff people. Or, use the Field Collection contributed module to create a staff field collection that is attached to the Company content type.

- You have a field collection use case similar to the Staff of Company example, but you feel that it is general enough that many other websites would want to use this same field collection. In this case, it makes sense to create a custom field module and contribute it to drupal.org so that others can use it.

Assuming that you have decided you need a custom field module, here is an overview of how to define a field type:

1. Implement hook_field_info() in your *mymodule.module* file to provide basic information about your field type (such as the label used to select it when attaching a field to an entity bundle in the administrative user interface).

2. Implement hook_field_schema() in your *mymodule.install* file to provide information about the data stored in your field. This defines database fields in a way similar to hook_schema(), but it is not exactly the same.

3. Set up a widget for editing the field, and a formatter for displaying it (see following sections).

There are many field modules that are freely available for download from drupal.org, so rather than providing another programming example here, I'll just suggest that you use one of the following as a starting point for finding examples of these two hooks in action:

- The Field example in the Examples for Developers project (*http://drupal.org/project/examples*), which has some extra documentation explaining what is going on.

- A Drupal core field module (Image, File, Text, List, Number, or Taxonomy, as of Drupal 7). The documentation for the two field hooks is also part of Drupal core, in the file *modules/field/field.api.php* (or look them up on *http://api.drupal.org*).

- Date, Link, or another contributed field module (search modules for category "Fields").

Drupal 8
The process of defining a field type is likely to change in Drupal 8, as the Field system is moving to the use of plugins.

Related topics in this book:

- "Programming with Hooks in Modules and Themes" (page 11)
- "Finding Drupal add-ons" (page 3)
- "Defining an Entity Type" (page 68)
- "Programming with Field Widgets" (page 77)
- "Programming with Field Formatters" (page 79)
- "Setting Up Database Tables: Schema API and hook_update_N()" (page 22)

Programming with Field Widgets

There are several reasons that you may need to do some programming with field widgets:

- If you have defined your own custom field type, you will need to define a widget for entering data for that field, or repurpose an existing widget for use on your field.
- You may need to define a custom input method for an existing field type.
- You may be want to repurpose an existing widget for use on a different field type.

Drupal 8
This is likely to change in Drupal 8, as the Field system is moving to the use of plugins.

Defining a field widget

To define a field widget, you need to implement two hooks in your *mymodule.module* file: hook_field_widget_info() and hook_field_widget_form(); the latter uses the Form API. If you're defining a field widget for a custom field type that you've defined, I suggest going back to the field type module you used as a starting point, and using that module's widget hook implementations as a starting point for your widget.

If you're defining a new widget for an existing field, the following example may be helpful: assume that you want to define a widget for the core Text field that provides a custom method for input of plain text data, which could use Flash, JavaScript, or an image map to let the user click on a region on an image or map, and store their choice as a predefined text string in the field. As a proxy for the custom code, this example just uses an HTML select element (although Drupal core provides a select list widget for text fields, so if that is all you need, don't define a custom widget). Here are the two hook implementations:

```
// Provide information about the widget.
function mymodule_field_widget_info() {
  return array(
    // Machine name of the widget.
    'mymodule_mywidget' => array(
      // Label for the administrative UI.
      'label' => t('Custom text input'),
      // Field types it supports.
      'field types' => array('text'),
    ),
    // Define additional widgets here, if desired.
  );
}

// Set up an editing form.
```

```
// Return a Form API form array.
function mymodule_field_widget_form(&$form, &$form_state, $field,
  $instance, $langcode, $items, $delta, $element) {

  // Verify the widget type.
  if ($instance['widget']['type'] == 'mymodule_mywidget') {
    // Find the current text field value.
    $value = isset($items[$delta]['value']) ? $items[$delta]['value'] : NULL;

    // Set up the editing form element. Substitute your custom
    // code here, instead of using an HTML select.
    $element += array(
      '#type' => 'select',
      '#options' => array('x' => 'x value', 'y' => 'y value'),
      '#default_value' => $value,
    );
  }

  return $element;
}
```

Related topics in this book:

- "Programming with Hooks in Modules and Themes" (page 11)
- "Generating Forms with the Form API" (page 59)

Repurposing an existing field widget

Since the module that defines the widget tells Drupal what field types it supports in its hook_field_widget_info() implementation, if you want to repurpose an existing widget to apply to a different field type, in your *mymodule.module* file, you need to implement hook_field_widget_info_alter(). This hook allows you to alter the information collected from all other modules' implementations of hook_widget_info_alter(). For example:

```
function mymodule_field_widget_info_alter(&$info) {
  // Add another field type to a widget.
  $info['widget_machine_name']['field types'][] = 'another_field_type';
}
```

You may also need to alter the widget form so that the widget will work correctly with the new field type. There are two "form alter" hooks that you can use for this: hook_field_widget_form_alter(), which gets called for all widget forms, and the more specific hook_field_widget_WIDGET_TYPE_form_alter(), which gets called only for the widget you are interested in (and is therefore preferable).

Further reading and references:

- "Programming with Hooks in Modules and Themes" (page 11)

- "Generating Forms with the Form API" (page 59)
- "Altering forms" (page 63)
- *http://api.drupal.org* is the best place to look up details of any of the hooks mentioned here.

Programming with Field Formatters

There are two reasons you might need to do some programming with field formatters:

- If you have defined your own custom field type, you will need to define a formatter that displays the data for that field, or re-purpose an existing field formatter.
- You may need to define a custom formatting method for an existing field type.

To define a field formatter, you need to implement two hooks in your *mymodule.module* file: `hook_field_formatter_info()` and `hook_field_formatter_view()`. If you're defining a field formatter for a custom field type that you've defined, I suggest going back to the field type module you used as a starting point, and using that module's formatter hook implementations as a starting point for your formatter. If you need to repurpose an existing field formatter for a different field type, use `hook_field_formatter_info_alter()`, which works the same as `hook_field_widget_info_alter()` described in the previous section.

If you're defining a new formatter for an existing field, the following example may be helpful: assume that you have set up a Text field with several preselected values, and on output, you want to display an icon or some predefined text that corresponds to the preselected value.

Here are the hook implementations for this formatter example:

```
// Provide information about the formatter.
function mymodule_field_formatter_info() {
  return array(
    // Machine name of the formatter.
    'mymodule_myformatter' => array(
      // Label for the administrative UI.
      'label' => t('Custom text output'),
      // Field types it supports.
      'field types' => array('text'),
    ),
    // Define additional formatters here.
  );
}

// Define how the field information is displayed.
// Return a render array.
function mymodule_field_formatter_view($entity_type, $entity,
```

```
  $field, $instance, $langcode, $items, $display) {
  $output = array();

  // Verify the formatter type.
  if ($display['type'] == 'mymodule_myformatter') {
    // Handle multi-valued fields.
    foreach ($items as $delta => $item) {
      // See which option was selected.
      switch ($item['value']) {
        case 'predefined_value_1':
          // Output the corresponding text or icon.
          $output[$delta] = array('#markup' => '<p>' .
            t('Predefined output text 1') . '</p>');
          break;

        // Handle other options here.
      }
    }
  }

  return $output;
}
```

Drupal 8
This is likely to change in Drupal 8, as the Field system is moving to the use of plugins.

Further reading, examples, and reference:

- Render arrays: "Providing Page and Block Output" (page 55)
- There are many Drupal core examples of field formatters. You can find the core implementations of hook_field_formatter_info() by looking this up on *http://api.drupal.org*.
- A contributed module that I wrote, Simple Google Maps (*http://drupal.org/project/simple_gmap*) is another good example to look at.
- The Field example from Examples for Developers (*http://drupal.org/project/examples*) is also good.

Creating Views Module Add-Ons

The contributed Views module is, at its heart, a query engine for Drupal that can be used to make formatted lists of pretty much any data stored in the Drupal database. The base Views module and other contributed Views add-on modules provide the ability to query Node module content items, comments, taxonomy terms, users, and other data;

to filter and sort the data in various ways; to relate one type of data to another; and to display the data using a list, table, map, and other formats. In addition, custom entities and fields that you have defined are well-supported by Views, and Views uses the Field system's formatters to display field data. But even with all of that ability, you may sometime have needs not covered by Views and existing add-on modules.

This section of the book provides an overview of how to create your own Views module add-ons for the following purposes:

- Querying additional types of data
- Relating new data to existing data types
- Formatting the output in additional ways
- Providing default Views that site builders can use directly or adapt to their needs

Each topic below is independent, except that they all depend on having your module set up so that Views recognizes it. So, start by reading "Views Programming Terminology and Output Construction" (page 81) and "Setting Up Your Module for Views" (page 82), and then skip to the section that you need. Also, some of the topics in this section assume knowledge of advanced usage of the Views user interface, such as relationships and contextual filters.

Further reading and references:

- Views module: *http://drupal.org/project/views*
- "Avoiding Custom Programming with Fielded Data" (page 39)
- "Programming with Entities and Fields" (page 66)
- For Views programming not covered in this book, there is documentation in the *views.api.php* file distributed with the Views module.

 Drupal 8

The Views module has been added to Drupal core in Drupal version 8, and in the process, it has adopted the Drupal 8 core plugin system. So, while the philosophy of the examples here will probably remain the same, the details will be somewhat different.

Views Programming Terminology and Output Construction

The Views module version 7.x-3.x uses the term *handler* to refer to a class that takes care of field display, sorting, filtering, contextual filtering, or relationships. In contrast, the term *plugin* in Views 7.x-3.x is used to denote a class related to the overall display of the View, and other classes that take care of the basic functions of Views. The distinction between handlers and plugins is somewhat arbitrary, but since they're declared and defined differently, it's important to know about.

Drupal 8
The terminology of plugins versus handlers described here will likely change in the Drupal 8 version of Views, which will be part of Drupal core and adopt the Drupal core plugin system.

Besides this terminology, in order to program effectively with Views, you also need to understand how Views uses handlers and plugins to construct its output. Here is a conceptual overview (the actual order of Views performing these steps may be a bit different):

1. Views takes all of the relationship, filter, and field definitions in the View and creates and executes a database query.

2. If the View uses fields, each field is run through its field display handler.

3. Each row in the database query result is run through a *row style plugin*, if one is in use. Row style plugins format the rows.

4. The formatted rows are handed off to the *style plugin*, which combines the rows into a larger output. The base Views module includes style plugins for HTML tables, HTML unordered lists, and so on, and each style plugin is compatible with a certain subset of row style plugins (for instance, an HTML list can use either a field row style or a row style that displays the entire entity, while an HTML table does not use a row style).

5. The formatted output is handed off to the overall *display* plugin; examples of display plugins are the standard Views Page, Block, and Feed displays.

Setting Up Your Module for Views

The first step in any Views-related programming is to make sure Views recognizes your module, by implementing the Views hook hook_views_api() in your *mymodule.module* file. To do that, you'll need to choose a location for some additional files; typically, you make a sub-directory called *views* in your module directory to hold all of the Views files, and if you are doing a lot of output formatting, optionally another sub-directory for the theme template files. The hook_views_api() implementation tells Views this information. For example:

```
function mymodule_views_api() {
  return array(
    // Which version of the Views API you are using. For Views 7.x-3.x, use 3.
    'api' => 3,
    // Where your additional Views directory is.
    'path' => drupal_get_path('module', 'mymodule') . '/views',
    // Where Views-related theme templates are located.
    'template path' => drupal_get_path('module', 'mymodule') .
      '/views/templates',
  );
}
```

Any files that contain Views hooks (see sections below) will also need to be added to your *mymodule.info* file:

```
files[] = views/mymodule.views.inc
```

In addition, if Views integration is fundamental to the functioning of your module, you can make Views a module requirement by adding the following line to your *mymodule.info* file:

```
dependencies[] = views
```

Finally, Views caches information from its hooks, so whenever you implement a new Views hook, modify a Views hook implementation, or add new Views-related files to your module, you need to clear the Views cache. You can do this on the Views advanced settings page, where you can also disable Views caching while you're developing; the Views cache is also cleared when you clear the main Drupal cache.

Further reading:

- "Programming with Hooks in Modules and Themes" (page 11)
- "The Drupal Cache" (page 6)

Providing a New Views Data Source

A common need in a custom module is to *integrate it with Views*, which is to say, to make the data managed by the module available to Views. If your data is stored in entities or fields, and you have used the Entity API module to define a custom entity or attached fields to an existing entity (whether they are Drupal core fields or fields that you have defined), then your data will be integrated with Views without any further work.

Alternatively, if your module stores its data in a custom database table, then you can integrate it with Views by defining a new Views *data source* (also known as a *base table*). The data source can then be selected when setting up a new View: instead of selecting a Node-module Content view (the default), you can select your data source instead, or if appropriate, you can create a View using one data type, and use a relationship to join it with your data type. Adding data sources is described in this section; the next section describes how to add fields and relationships to existing data sources.

To define a Views data source, assuming you have already followed the steps in "Setting Up Your Module for Views" (page 82), start by creating a file called *mymodule.views.inc*, which must be located in the Views directory specified in your hook_views_api() implementation. In this file, implement hook_views_data(). The return value of this hook is an associative array of arrays, where the outermost array key is the database table name, and the array value gives information about that database table, the way it relates to other data tables known to Views, and the database table fields that can be used for filtering, sorting, and field display. Here is an example showing a working subset of the return value of this hook, which I wrote for the contributed API module:

```
// The table name from hook_schema() is 'api_documentation'.
$data['api_documentation'] = array(
  // Information about the table itself.
  'table' => array(
    // Group used for the fields in this table.
    'group' => t('API documentation'),
    'base' => array(
      // The primary key of this table.
      'field' => 'did',
      // The label shown when selecting this table in Views.
      'title' => t('API documentation'),
      'help' => t('API documentation objects'),
      'weight' => 20,
    ),
  ),

  // Information about the primary key field. It cannot be used
  // for display, filter, or sorting.
  'did' => array(
    'title' => t('Documentation ID'),
    // Relationship with the Comment table.
    'relationship' => array(
      'base' => 'comment',
      // Field in the comment table that corresponds to this field.
      'base field' => 'nid',
      'handler' => 'views_handler_relationship',
      'label' => t('Comments'),
      'title' => t('All comments'),
      'help' => t('All comments on the documentation object'),
    ),
  ),

  // Another field.
  'object_name' => array(
```

```
      'title' => t('Object name'),
      'help' => t('Name of this object'),
      // How this field can be used for display.
      'field' => array(
        // This uses a custom field display handler class.
        'handler' => 'api_views_handler_field_api_linkable',
        'click sortable' => TRUE,
      ),
      // Sorting is handled by the generic Views sort handler.
      'sort' => array(
        'handler' => 'views_handler_sort',
        'click sortable' => TRUE,
      ),
      // Filtering is handled by the generic Views string filter handler.
      'filter' => array(
        'handler' => 'views_handler_filter_string',
      ),
      // Contextual filtering (formerly known as using an "argument")
      // is handled by the generic Views string argument handler.
      'argument' => array(
        'handler' => 'views_handler_argument_string',
      ),
    ),
  );
```

Your hook_views_data() implementation refers to the names of handler classes for field display, filtering, sorting, and contextual filtering. You have the choice to use the standard handler classes provided by the Views module (located in the *handlers* subdirectory of the Views download) or a class you create. To create your own handler class, here are the steps:

1. Create a *handlers* subdirectory inside the Views directory specified in your hook_views_api() implementation.

2. In that subdirectory, create an include file named for your handler class, such as *mymodule_views_handler_field_myfield.inc* if your class is called mymodule_views_handler_field_myfield. Note that in contrast with the usual Drupal coding standards, for historical reasons Views-related classes are generally defined using all lowercase names with underscores, rather than CamelCase names.

3. In that file, extend an existing Views handler class of the same type (field, filter, and so on), and override the appropriate methods to define the actions of your class. For instance, if you are making a field handler, you'll need to extend the views_handler_field class, and override the render() method; if your field handler has display options, you'll also need to override the option_definition() and options_form() methods.

4. Add the handler file to your *mymodule.info* file:

   ```
   files[] = views/handlers/mymodule_views_handler_field_myfield.inc
   ```

Further reading, examples, and references:

- "Programming with Entities and Fields" (page 66)
- "Setting Up Database Tables: Schema API and hook_update_N()" (page 22)
- The Views module's *handlers* directory contains general purpose handlers. Use these as starting points when defining your own handlers.
- The API module also has some good examples of handler classes: *http://drupal.org/ project/api*

Adding Fields and Relationships to an Existing Views Data Source

In addition to providing completely new Views data sources, as described in the previous section, some custom modules may need to provide additional fields or relationships to existing Views data sources. A common use case would be that your module adds some data to Node module content items, and you would like this data to be available to Views defined on the Node table, either as a field or through a relationship. This section tells you how to accomplish telling Views about your additional data; it assumes you have already followed the steps in "Setting Up Your Module for Views" (page 82).

To add a field or relationship to an existing Views data source, implement `hook_views_data_alter()` in your *mymodule.views.inc* file, which must be located in the Views directory specified in your `hook_views_api()` implementation. This hook takes as its argument, by reference, the array of information returned by all modules' `hook_views_data()` implementations, so that your module can alter or add to the information.

This example from the API module illustrates the two most common things you can do with this hook:

- Adding a relationship from an existing table to your table. In this example, the reason is that the API module allows users to comment on API documentation pages, so if someone was creating a view whose base data source was comments, they might want to add a relationship to the API documentation page that was being commented upon. Relationships are defined on the base table side, so this relationship needs to be added to the comment data source.
- Adding an existing automatic join to your table (automatic joins provide additional database fields to a data source without having to add a relationship to the View). Again, this example is comment-related: the `node_comment_statistics` table is normally automatically joined to the `node` base table, so that the number-of-comments field is available on node content items. This example adds the automatic join to the `api_documentation` base table as well.

Here is the code:

```
function api_views_data_alter(&$data) {
  // Add a relationship to the Comment table.
  $data['comment']['did'] = array(
    'title' => t('Documentation ID'),
    'help' => t('The ID of the documentation object the comment is a reply to.'),
    'relationship' => array(
      // Table to join to.
      'base' => 'api_documentation',
      // Field in that table to join with.
      'base field' => 'did',
      // Field in the comment table to join with.
      'field' => 'nid',
      'handler' => 'views_handler_relationship',
      'label' => t('API documentation object'),
      'title' => t('API documentation object'),
      'help' => t('The ID of the documentation object the comment is a reply to.'),
    ),
  );

  // Add an automatic join between the comment statistics table and
  // the API documentation table.
  $data['node_comment_statistics']['table']['join']['api_documentation'] =
    array(
      // Use an inner join.
      'type' => 'INNER',
      // Field to join on in the API documentation table.
      'left_field' => 'did',
      // Field to join on in the comment statistics table.
      'field' => 'nid',
    );
}
```

Providing a Display Plugin to Views

Another common custom Views programming need is to create new style or row style plugins. Here are the steps you'll need to follow, assuming you have already followed the steps in "Setting Up Your Module for Views" (page 82):

1. Implement hook_views_plugins() in your *mymodule.views.inc* file, which must be located in the Views directory specified in your hook_views_api() implementation. The return value tells Views about your style and row style plugin classes. For instance, you might have:

```
function mymodule_views_plugins() {
  return array(
    // Overall style plugins
    'style' => array(
```

```
     // First style plugin--machine name is the array key.
     'mymodule_mystyle' => array(
       // Information about this plugin.
       'title' => t('My module my style'),
       'help' => t('Longer description goes here'),
       // The class for this plugin and where to find it.
       'handler' => 'mymodule_views_plugin_style_mystyle',
       'path' => drupal_get_path('module', 'mymodule') . '/views/plugins',
       // Some settings.
       'uses row plugin' => TRUE,
       'uses fields' => TRUE,
     ),

     // Additional style plugins go here.
   ),

   // Row style plugins.
   'row' => array(
     // First row style plugin -- machine name is the array key.
     'mymodule_myrowstyle' => array(
       // Information about this plugin.
       'title' => t('My module my row style'),
       'help' => t('Longer description goes here'),
       // The class for this plugin and where to find it.
       'handler' => 'mymodule_views_plugin_row_myrowstyle',
       'path' => drupal_get_path('module', 'mymodule') . '/views/plugins',
       // Some settings.
       'uses fields' => TRUE,
     ),

     // Additional row style plugins go here.
   ),
 );
}
```

2. Create a file for each style or row style plugin class. For example, if you declared that your class is called mymodule_views_plugin_style_mystyle, create a file with the name *mymodule_views_plugin_style_mystyle.inc*. Put this file in the directory you specified in your hook_views_plugins() implementation (typically, plugins are either put into your Views directory or a subdirectory called *plugins*).

3. List each class-containing include file in your *mymodule.info* file, with a line like:

```
files[] = views/plugins/mymodule_views_plugin_style_mystyle.inc
```

4. In each class-containing include file, declare your plugin class, which should extend either the views_plugin_style, views_plugin_row, or another subclass of these

classes. You will need to override the `option_definition()` and `options_form()` methods, if your plugin has options, and (oddly enough), that is usually all you'll need to override, because the work of formatting the output is done in the theme layer.

5. Set up `hook_theme()` to define a theme template and preprocessing function for your plugin. The theme template goes into the template directory specified in your `hook_views_info()` implementation, and the name corresponds to the machine name you gave your plugin (in this example, *mymodule-mystyle.tpl.php* or *mymodule-myrowstyle.tpl.php*).

Further reading and examples of plugin classes:

- "Making Your Output Themeable" (page 13)
- The Views module itself has several general purpose plugin examples (*http://drupal.org/project/views*). The `hook_views_plugins()` implementation is in the file *includes/plugins.inc*. The plugin class files are in the directory *plugins* and are named *views_plugin_style*.inc* and *views_plugin_row*.inc*. The template files (named with the array keys from the hook implementation) are in the *theme* directory, and theme preprocessing functions are in the file *theme.inc* in the *theme* directory.
- There are several contributed module projects that provide Views plugin add-ons. Commonly used examples are Views Data Export (*http://drupal.org/project/views_data_export*), Calendar (*http://drupal.org/project/calendar*), and Views Slideshow (*http://drupal.org/project/views_slideshow*). You can find others by browsing category "Views" at *http://drupal.org/project/modules* (but note that only some of the Views-related modules in that list provide style or row plugins).

Providing Default Views

Once you have your module's data integrated with Views, either because it is stored in entities using the Entity API module, core entities, or fields or because you have provided a custom data source as described in sections above, you may want to supply users of your module with one or more default Views. These Views can be used to provide administration pages for your module or sample output pages, and they can either be enabled by default or disabled by default (administrators can enable and modify them as needed).

Here are the steps to follow to provide one or more default Views in your module, assuming you have already followed the steps in "Setting Up Your Module for Views" (page 82):

1. Create a View using the Views user interface.

2. From the Views user interface, export the View. This will give you some PHP code starting with `$view = new view;`.

3. If you want to have the View disabled by default, find the line near the top that says `$view->disabled = FALSE;` and change it to `TRUE`.

4. Implement `hook_views_default_views()` in a file called *mymodule.views_default.inc*, which must be located in the Views directory specified in your `hook_views_api()` implementation.

5. Put the exported Views' PHP code into this hook implementation:

```
function mymodule_views_default_views() {
  // We'll return this array at the end.
  $views = array();

  // Exported view code starts here.
  $view = new view;
  // ... rest of exported code ...
  // Exported code ends here.

  // Add this view to the return array.
  $views[$view->name] = $view;

  // You can add additional exported views here.

  return $views;
}
```

Related topics:

- "Programming with Entities and Fields" (page 66)

Creating Rules Module Add-Ons

The contributed Rules module lets you set up *actions* to respond to *events* under certain *conditions* on your website. For example, you could respond to a new comment submission event, under the condition that the submitter is an anonymous user, by sending the comment moderator an email message. The Rules module also gives you the ability to combine conditions via Boolean and/or logic, so that you can be quite specific about when to respond to a given event when configuring Rules (again, without any programming on your part). Furthermore, Rules actions can have parameter inputs and they can provide data outputs; this means that you can chain actions together, with the output data provided by one action feeding in as a parameter for the next action. It is also possible within Rules to loop actions, so if an action provides a list as output, you can execute a single-parameter action for each data item in the list.

The Rules module comes with a set of standard events, conditions, and actions, including (via integration with the Entity API module) many related to entities and fields. This means that if your module stores its custom data in an entity or fields, you will be able to use Rules with your module's data without any further programming. But you may occasionally find that you need to do some programming to add additional functionality to the Rules module; in my experience, this has always been to add custom actions to Rules; this is described in "Providing Custom Actions to Rules" (page 91).

Rules that you compose using the Rules user interface can be exported into PHP code and shared with others. One way to do this is by using the Features contributed module. But sometimes Features is cumbersome, and there is a direct method for exporting and sharing Rules described in "Providing Default Rules" (page 93) below.

Further reading and references:

- Rules module: *http://drupal.org/project/rules*
- Features module: *http://drupal.org/project/features*
- "Programming with Entities and Fields" (page 66)
- For programming with Rules not covered in this book, see the *rules.api.php* file distributed with the Rules module for documentation. For instance, it is possible to set up custom conditions and events, although it is unlikely you will ever need to, given the flexibility of the base Rules module.

Providing Custom Actions to Rules

Rules actions are responses to events and conditions detected by the Rules module, and they can take many forms. Built-in actions that come with the Rules module include sending an email message, displaying a message or warning, and altering content (publishing, unpublishing, etc.). As mentioned in the introduction to this section, you can chain together the input and output of several actions and you can also use action output for looping, so some so-called "actions" in Rules are really more like processing steps that exist solely to provide input for other actions that are actually doing the work (modifying content, sending email, etc.).

Whether you are defining a processing step type of action or one that actually does work itself, here are the steps you will need to follow to provide a custom action to the Rules module:

1. Create a file called *mymodule.rules.inc* in your main module directory, and implement `hook_rules_action_info()` in that file. The return value tells Rules about your custom action: its machine name, a human-readable label for the Rules user interface, the data that it requires as parameters (if any), and the data that it provides as output (if any).

2. Create a callback function that executes your action. You can either put this function in your *mymodule.rules.inc* file, or you can implement `hook_rules_file_info()` and specify a separate include file for callbacks. The name of the function is the same as the machine name you gave the action.

As an example, here is the code to provide a processing-step-type action that takes a content item as input, and outputs a list of users (you could then loop over the output list and send each user an email message, for instance):

```
// Optional hook_rules_file_info() implementation.
// This specifies a separate file for callback functions.
// It goes into mymodule.rules.inc.
function mymodule_rules_file_info() {
  // Leave off the .inc file name suffix.
  return array('mymodule.rules-callbacks');
}

// Required hook_rules_action_info() implementation.
// This gives information about your action.
// It goes into mymodule.rules.inc.
function mymodule_rules_action_info() {
  $actions = array();

  // Define one action.
  // The array key is the machine name of the action.
  $actions['mymodule_rules_action_user_list'] = array(
    // Label and group in the user interface.
    'label' => t('Load a list of users related to content'),
    'group' => t('Mymodule custom'),
    // Describe the parameter.
    'parameter' => array(
      'item' => array(
        'label' => t('Content item to use'),
        // Entity type (Node module).
        'type' => 'node',
        // Restrict to a particular content type.
        // (optional)
        'bundles' => array('my_content_type'),
      ),
      // You can add additional parameters here.
    ),
    // Describe the output.
    'provides' => array(
      'user_list' => array(
        'type' => 'list<user>',
        'label' => t('List of users related to content'),
      ),
      // You could describe additional output here.
    ),
  );
```

```
  // Define other actions here.

  return $actions;
}

// Required callback function that performs the action.
// This goes in mymodule.rules.inc, or the file defined in
// the optional hook_rules_file_info() implementation.
// The function name is the action's machine name.
function mymodule_rules_action_user_list($item) {
  // Read some information from $item.
  // ...
  // Do some query to relate this to user IDs.
  // ...

  // As a proxy for your real code, return a list of one
  // user -- the author of the content.
  $ids = array($item->uid);

  // Load the users and return them to Rules.
  return array('user_list' => user_load_multiple($ids));
}
```

Further reading:

- "Programming with Hooks in Modules and Themes" (page 11)

Providing Default Rules

In some cases, you may find that you want to put Rules you have created into PHP code, so that you can use them on another site. You have three choices for how to do this:

- Define the Rule's event, conditions, and reactions using pure PHP code. This is somewhat documented in the *rules.api.php* file distributed with the Rules module, but is not particularly recommended, since you'll need to read a lot of Rules module code to figure out the machine names of all the components your rule needs to use, and there isn't really any documentation on how to put it all together.

- Create the Rule using the Rules user interface, and use the contributed Features module to manage the export.

- Create the Rule using the Rules user interface, export the rule definition to a text file, and use the rules_import() function to read it into code. This process is recommended if you do not want to use the Features module; the process is described in the coming section.

Assuming you want to use the export-to-text option, here are the steps to follow:

1. In the Rules user interface, create your Rule. If you do not want the rule to be active by default, be sure to deactivate it.

2. From the main page of the Rules user interface, export your rule, and save the exported text in a file. Put this file in a subdirectory *rules* of your main module directory, and name it *sample_rule.txt* (for example).

3. Implement `hook_default_rules_configuration()` in a file named *mymodule.rules_defaults.inc*, with the following code:

```
function mymodule_default_rules_configuration() {
  $configs = array();

  // Read in one exported Rule.
  $file = drupal_get_path('module', 'mymodule') . '/rules/sample_rule.txt';
  $contents = file_get_contents($file);
  $configs['mymodule_sample_rule'] = rules_import($contents);

  // Add other Rules here if desired.

  return $configs;
}
```

Further reading and references:

- Features module: *http://drupal.org/project/features*
- "Programming with Hooks in Modules and Themes" (page 11)

CHAPTER 5

Programming Tools and Tips

As you launch yourself into (or continue) what will hopefully be many productive years as a Drupal programmer, I hope that you will continue to keep the principles of Chapter 2 in mind and avoid the mistakes listed in Chapter 3. You should be able to keep returning to Chapter 4 and outside references such as the Examples for Developers project (*http://drupal.org/project/examples*) for examples and ideas. And for further study, there are suggestions sprinkled throughout this book and in "Where to Find More Information" (page vii).

In closing, I'd like to offer a few final programming tips and suggest a few development tools that you should find useful in your endeavors.

Drupal Development Tools

The Drupal community has developed several very useful development tools that can help you avoid making programming mistakes, adhere to the Drupal coding standards, and debug your Drupal sites and Drupal code. Here is a list of the most useful development tools:

Coder
> A set of modules that points out coding errors and violations of the Drupal coding standards, and also helps you upgrade your code from one Drupal version to another. Some developers have, in the past, preferred to use the Drupal Code Sniffer project, which has now been merged into the Coder project. (*http://drupal.org/ project/coder*)

Devel
> A set of modules containing a number of helpful functions for debugging and developing modules and themes, as well as a fake *lorem ipsum* content generator for testing. (*http://drupal.org/project/devel*)

Drupal for Firebug

A Firefox/Firebug or Chrome web browser plugin that works with the Devel module to display information about how each Drupal-generated page was built. (*http://drupal.org/project/drupalforfirebug*)

Drush

A project that provides a command-line shell that greatly speeds up the process of developing a site, with commands for downloading and installing modules, clearing the Drupal cache, and more. It also has an API for module developers that lets a module expose its administrative functions as Drush commands. Learning a few key Drush commands will save you a lot of time, because in one command and a few seconds of waiting, you can do things that would otherwise take you several clicks and page loads on a site's administrative interface. (*http://drupal.org/project/drush*)

Coding standards

It is a very good idea to follow the Drupal coding standards in your Drupal programming. This practice has several benefits:

- It makes your code more uniform, matching the style of existing Drupal core and contributed module code.
- It makes your code easier to read and maintain going forward.
- If you plan to contribute your code to the Drupal project, it will eventually need to comply with these standards, so it's best to start now.

Further reading and references:

- "The Drupal Cache" (page 6)
- Drupal project coding standards: *http://drupal.org/coding-standards*

Finding Drupal API Functions

Programmers who are new to Drupal sometimes don't know about all of the useful functions available to them in the Drupal API. Most PHP programmers know that they can go to *http://php.net* to find documentation on built-in PHP functions; the Drupal project has a similar API site at *http://api.drupal.org*, which lists all of the functions, constants, classes, and files in Drupal core.

Using api.drupal.org

The website *http://api.drupal.org* is an invaluable reference for Drupal programmers (note: I may be biased in thinking this, since I currently maintain the software that the site runs on and am also the Drupal core committer/maintainer for API documentation). Several contributed Drupal modules also run API reference sites that use the same software.

Here are some features that you can take advantage of; not all of them may be available on all API reference sites, depending on what version of the API software they are running:

- Every Drupal core file, class, constant, and function ("item") has a page on the site. As of this writing, there are plans to include all of the contributed modules on this site as well, but until that happens, the site *http://drupalcontrib.org* (which runs the same software and attempts to include all contributed modules) can be used.

- Most items are well-documented and most of the documentation is accurate. The documentation is built from comments in the source code, so it tends to be updated when code is updated. (If you find a problem, you can click a link on the page to report an issue.)

- You can search directly for a function, class, or constant name, if you know it.

- Topic pages provide additional documentation about the Drupal API: explanations and a list of related functions and classes. If you do not know the name of the specific Drupal function or class you want to use, try browsing the Topics list.

- The source code of each item is shown, so if the documentation is unclear, you can read the code to see what's really going on.

- Hooks (places where modules can alter the Drupal core behavior) are also documented. The function body of hook documentation gives a sample hook implementation.

- There is a lot of cross-linking:
  - File pages show all items defined in the file, and items link to their file. So if you are on a function page and want to find related functions, click on the file link to see what else is defined in the same file.

— Topic pages show related items, and items link to topics. So if you are on a function page and it has a related topics link, try that link to find related functions.

— Items in code listings link to their pages.

— Each function page has a link to a page showing all the places in Drupal core that call the function. There are also pages showing string references to functions, where hooks are invoked, and hook implementations.

— Classes and interfaces have hierarchy listings, showing which classes extend or implement them.

I'll also just mention that a lot of really useful functions are defined in files *common.inc* and *bootstrap.inc* in the *includes* directory of Drupal core. You can search for either file on the API site; browsing their function lists is a great way to familiarize yourself with what's available in the Drupal API. You might also want to browse the Topics list on the API site, to get an idea of what general areas of functionality the API covers.

Finally, here is a list, in order, of the 20 most-often-called functions within Drupal core version 7 (you might want to learn about them):

- t()
- variable_get()
- db_query()
- variable_set()
- url()
- drupal_set_message()
- db_select()
- theme()
- db_update()
- drupal_static()
- check_plain()
- drupal_get_path()
- db_delete()
- user_access()
- db_insert()
- module_invoke_all()

- `l()`
- `watchdog()`
- `drupal_static_reset()`
- `drupal_alter()`

Other Programming Tips and Suggestions

Here are a few final suggestions that will help you improve your Drupal code and programming experience:

- Set up your own local development server with a LAMP stack (or WAMP, MAMP, and so on), rather than trying to develop using a remote server.

- On your development server, edit your php.ini file (or equivalent) so that you are displaying all PHP notices, warnings, and errors. Do not consider your code to be working unless there are no notices at all, since they generally indicate bugs. Also use the Database Logging module during development, and check the "Recent log messages" report to see any errors you might have missed.

- Get a good code editor that does syntax highlighting, automatic indenting, and parentheses matching. The classic editor choices are Emacs and Vim/Vi; some people prefer to use Integrated Development Environments such as NetBeans, Eclipse, and Komodo.

- Follow the Drupal coding standards. You should be able to set up your code editor to use the standard Drupal indentation practice (2 spaces, never use tabs), and to display or remove extra end-of-line spaces.

- Write thorough documentation for every function, constant, and class that you define, preferably before you write the code. This will help you or others maintain your code going forward, and writing the documentation first will help ensure that you know what the function or class is really supposed to do before you start writing it.

- Test your code, preferably by writing automated tests.

- Use a revision control system, such as Git or Subversion, to keep track of the changes you make to modules and themes you develop.

Further reading and references:

- Drupal coding standards: *http://drupal.org/coding-standards*
- "Principle: Drupal Code Is Tested and Documented" (page 31)

About the Author

Jennifer Hodgdon wrote her first computer program in 1982, and has been a professional software developer since 1994, using a wide variety of programming languages (FORTRAN, C, Java, PHP, JavaScript, ...). She started doing PHP/MySQL web programming professionally around 2002, and set up her first Drupal website in 2007. Soon after that, she started contributing volunteer time to the Drupal open-source project and the Seattle Drupal User Group: organizing meet-ups and conferences, serving as the co-leader and then the leader of the Drupal Documentation Team in 2011-2012, leading workshops, and making conference presentations. She is currently a freelance Drupal site builder and module programmer, the volunteer maintainer of several Drupal modules, the co-organizer of the Spokane Washington Drupal User Group, and the Drupal core maintainer/committer for API documentation and coding standards. She can be contacted through her business website, poplarware.com, or through her Drupal.org user account (jhodgdon).

Have it your way.

Get even more for your money.

Join the O'Reilly Community, and register the O'Reilly books you own. It's free, and you'll get:

- $4.99 ebook upgrade offer
- 40% upgrade offer on O'Reilly print books
- Membership discounts on books and events
- Free lifetime updates to ebooks and videos
- Multiple ebook formats, DRM FREE
- Participation in the O'Reilly community
- Newsletters
- Account management
- 100% Satisfaction Guarantee

Signing up is easy:

1. **Go to: oreilly.com/go/register**
2. **Create an O'Reilly login.**
3. **Provide your address.**
4. **Register your books.**

Note: English-language books only

To order books online:

oreilly.com/store

For questions about products or an order:

orders@oreilly.com

To sign up to get topic-specific email announcements and/or news about upcoming books, conferences, special offers, and new technologies:

elists@oreilly.com

For technical questions about book content:

booktech@oreilly.com

To submit new book proposals to our editors:

proposals@oreilly.com

O'Reilly books are available in multiple DRM-free ebook formats. For more information:

oreilly.com/ebooks

O'REILLY®